Americanata

Three Sisters in Italy, 1938

Becky Landrum and Mike Landrum

Printed in the United States of America

Hardcover ISBN: 978-1-961624-49-8
Paperback ISBN: 978-1-961624-50-4
Ebook ISBN: 978-1-961624-38-2

Canoe Tree Press

Canoe Tree Press is a division of DartFrog Books
301 S. McDowell St.
Suite 125-1625
Charlotte, NC 28204
www.DartFrogBooks.com

"There is no duty we so much underrate as the duty of being happy."
—*Robert Louis Stevenson*

For my children and grandchildren...and theirs.

Contents

Foreword

In 1997 Becky Fahrig Landrum was 80 years old. Stuart M. Landrum, her loyal husband of more than fifty-seven years, had just passed away a few days before. There had been a large group of friends and neighbors at his funeral crowding into 503 West College St. Farmington Missouri, their home for over forty years.

A week or two later, Becky went to her desk in the living room and from the bottom drawer, she pulled out a small, tattered book with the words, "Scribble Book" embossed in gold on the faded red cover. She also got out a fat, white scrapbook. On its cover, hand-printed in black Magic Marker, were the words, "Becky's Trip to Italy 1938."

Mike & Becky Landrum

This scrapbook had been her refuge. Not simply the collection from the trip, it had been transformed over the years. The white heavy cardboard covers with the Magic Marker printing was too recent to be from some 1930's dime store. It was held together with three large bolts fitted into aluminum bolt covers, devices perhaps invented in the 1970's. The pages, 25 large clear plastic covers, like clear envelopes, each fat with contents, including the original brown paper pages from a cheap old-fashioned scrapbook. Each of the dozens of mementoes was pasted neatly onto the brown paper pages. Notes were written next to each keepsake in Mom's lovely, clear handwriting with a ball-point pen. This scrapbook was clearly a cherished piece of work, occupying many hours over the decades, and kept respectfully hidden from her husband.

In the fall of 1997, having buried her faithful and loving husband

Stu, she called me up in New York and said, "Now, it's time to write the book. Will you help me?" After more than sixty years, she wanted to share her adventure with the world. Our collaboration was simple. She remembered the events and I wrote them down. Nearly three years later, in early 2001, we sent it to a publisher and she began a happy period of sharing and enjoying publicly the memories and experiences that had been her private joy for over sixty years.

Of course, publication of the memoir had stimulated more memories; the recollections of old friends, relatives, letters, and Mom herself. The old stories continued to expand. Now, eleven years after Becky's passing at the age of 95, I've decided to flesh out some of those original, private memories and re-publish her memoir. Becky Fahrig Landrum was a remarkable person and it has been a great privilege to be her son, to love her, and to bring her forever young spirit back into the world.

Mike

Michael Fahrig Landrum

Preface

Everyone begins with their parents, and so shall I. My mother, Florence June Short, was born on June 25, 1886, and brought up in Superior, Wisconsin, the daughter of the Presbyterian minister. She went through college and received a teacher's degree. In the fall of 1906, she got a job teaching first grade in the small town of Washburn, Wisconsin, 85 miles east of Superior on Chequamegon Bay at the southwestern tip of Lake Superior.

On the first day of her new job, she sent a note home with each of her students that read: "Hello. My name is Florence Short, and I am your child's first grade teacher." One little boy, Dwight Benton, took the note home but instead of giving it to his mother he gave it to his uncle, Harry H. Fahrig, saying, "Uncle Harry, this is what the teacher sent to you." Harry had been born December 25, 1882 and raised in Washburn and was at that time 23 years old and single. When little Dwight handed him the note, Harry happened to be standing on the porch of their house talking to one of his fellow workers from the nearby du Pont chemical plant. It soon got around that young Harry was receiving mash notes from the new schoolmarm and he had to put up with considerable joshing at work.

Du Pont was the source of most culture in Washburn and they regularly held socials, picnics and dances for the people of the town. At the first dance of the autumn that year Harry walked up to Florence and said, "I got your message." That was how my parents met. They were married October 16, 1907. If I had to describe them in a single word it would be 'natural' in the sense that they were without pretension. She seldom wore makeup, always wore her dark brown hair pulled into a bun, and carried her values and adornments in her mind. He was tall, slender as a rail and quietly capable of making anything with his hands. My father was proud of her and coined the phrase that "she had grown up in Superior with a Superior mind." That became the favorite definition of all of us children when thinking of her. After all, she completed four years of high school and four years of college in only four years—another fact we all knew and repeated with pride.

As a young lad Harry had been apprenticed to a cabinet maker. But when his father suddenly died in 1902, Harry, nineteen years old, became the family breadwinner, supporting his widowed mother and his younger sister. He accepted this early responsibility with a graceful maturity and left cabinet making to become a simple janitor for the du Pont Company in the dynamite plant just outside Washburn. He would work for du Pont for the rest of his life. A naturally gifted tinkerer and mechanic, he quickly made himself more useful at the plant, fixing and soon devising machinery. He studied vigorously and over the years taught himself engineering, rising in the company until he was the only staff member without a college education. My parents had a loving relationship as a couple, filled with respect and deference to each other.

Florence soon left the teaching job to raise their four children. In 1908, Harriet was born; Dick in 1910; Blossom in 1914; and I was born in 1917. I was the only one not born in Wisconsin. I had the distinction of being the first girl born in that tiny town of Ramsey, Montana. The du Pont Company had moved Daddy there to help build a new plant nine miles outside of Butte, to provide dynamite to the copper mines. Copper was needed for the First World War. When the war was over in 1919, we were sent back to Wisconsin.

The du Pont Company owned a lot of the homes in Washburn, ours included. With a total population of about 2500, it was an ideal place to be a child. The seasons were magically emphatic. Hot, green summer days buzzing with insects and wildflowers; snapping cold winters with the snow coming not in blankets so much as thick, feathery quilts. We lived there until I was eight. Those are luscious, long years in my memory—filled with light and a carefree joy.

The Fahrig family circa 1922 in Washburn, Wisconsin

A night that stands out in my mind was in the winter I was five. After the evening meal, my father had to walk to a distant neighbor's house to get some potatoes and he asked Blossom and me to go with him. Mother bundled us into leggings, galoshes that had side-buckles and came half way up our legs, heavy coats, stocking caps, mittens on a string of yarn that went through each sleeve so we couldn't lose them, and wool scarves wrapped around our necks and over our faces leaving only our eyes exposed. Thus prepared for the cold night air, we sat on our sled, a beautiful new Red Ryder, and Daddy began to pull us over the smooth, snow-covered streets several blocks to get the potatoes.

The evening was moonless, the air was cold, still and sparkling clear. There were no streetlights in our little town and stars in the millions glittered close overhead against the velvety black sky. It was probably my earliest extended look at them, and I gazed up in wonder. Our breath came like steam through our scarves. The only sound was the crunch and squeak of Father's footsteps and the hissing runners of our sled in the snow. Blossom and I waited the few minutes it took Daddy to get the potatoes, pay for them and bring the big burlap bag back to the sled. The night was bitter cold, so to keep the potatoes from freezing he had the two of us sit on the bag to keep it warm. We had a lap-robe around our legs that we tucked under the potatoes keeping them as toasty and snug as we were.

Some memories of childhood have an indelible power -- their vivid poignancy can be recalled to give us pleasure again and again. That winter evening is just such a memory for me. Blossom on the sled behind me, her arms around my waist; Daddy's strong back before us, pulling us over the crackling snow; the lumpy potatoes beneath us and the distinct stars overhead—this memory gives me still a feeling of safety and joy.

Summer in our small town in the early 1920's was a child's paradise. The season often started with Blossom bragging to me that Mother had allowed her to take off her long underwear. These garments were one-piece woolen affairs with legs that came to our shoe tops. They were itchy and uncomfortable but necessary for six months of the year. After a few days' wear they got very loose around our ankles and had to be rolled up in order to get our long stockings over them. This gave our slender little legs the lumpy bulk of hockey players. The day we could take them off was a celebration; it was a sign of Spring.

We lived in a duplex at the end of a street across from Lord's Orchard. We had a marvelous view of Lake Superior. We children were completely free to wander the meadows beyond our house or pick green apples from the orchard. The fears and anxieties that beset the modern family were completely unknown to us. Our pleasures were simple: a large vegetable garden for my father; my mother played the piano for church and at home we would gather round her at the keyboard and sing. In the evenings she would read to us. Sometimes a story—Pinocchio or

Ivanhoe would cause me such emotion of sadness that I wanted to cry. As the youngest I didn't want the family to see me teary, perhaps to tease me. So, I would run to the bathroom until I had collected myself enough to rejoin them for the rest of the story.

The family car was a Buick, a large, open touring model, which my father spent many hours tinkering with and fixing. Sometimes we drove to my grandparents' in Superior for a visit. Mother always packed a picnic lunch and we never drove the ninety miles of mostly gravel roads without several flat tires. When this happened, everybody would get out, daddy would pull the jack out of the toolbox attached to the running board. When the wheel was off the car and the tire was off the wheel and the inner tube pulled out, we kids would crowd around to see where the hole was. Daddy had to tell us all the time to "Get back, get back." In the toolbox was a little kit containing patches, some adhesive and an abrasive to rough up the rubber around the hole to so the patch would stick. Then he would apply the patch with glue, smooth it down, pump air into the inner tube with a little hand pump, put the tube back into the tire and the tire back onto the wheel. He was very adept at this, having done it so many times, but still, it took half an hour before we were on our way again.

One of the delights at Grandmother Short's house was the phonograph that sat in the living room, its fluted funnel raised into the air like a huge purple flower. I remember the thrill of being allowed, at last, to wind it up, set the delicate wooden needle carefully on the spinning black disk and bring a fountain of music into the room.

In 1924 Dad bought a new car, a beautiful long maroon Studebaker. It had open sides of course, with curtains that could be snapped on. The seats were leather, and the steering wheel was thick hardwood. The space between the front and back seats was so large that Blossom and I could make a tent with the lap robe and play house there. It was this car that I learned to drive when I was 14 years old. By that time, we had moved to Joplin where the garage had a narrow door, facing an equally narrow alley with a telephone pole just across from the garage door. We were allowed to use the car if we would put it away, backing it into the garage. The skill with which I learned to do that has left me comfortable backing into small places ever since.

We were a thrifty family of modest means. The rule of our house was: "Use it up, wear it out, make it do or do without." Daddy could fix everything, of course, and mother sewed the clothes for us girls. When we were little, she made us smocked dresses with bloomers to match. Later, for our first teen parties, we had organdy dresses with ruffles cut on the bias—yards and yards of hems which Mother carefully rolled by hand.

Washburn was very much a company town and the families with du Pont became fast friends. Mother and Dad always helped the young newcomers get acquainted. Once, Marcella, one of the young du Ponts came. Mother took her around the town, introducing her to the merchants who were awestruck by her name. She lived not far from us, and one day asked Dick, Blossom and me to lunch. I was very much impressed with the food—except for some funny white stuff in the fruit salad which I pushed aside untouched. Afterward Dick commented how good the marshmallows in the fruit salad were. I was sick that I had missed that good treat and never again left any new thing to eat without at least trying it.

In 1925 we were transferred to Joplin, Missouri, about which, I am sure, my father was somewhat ambivalent. It was a promotion, but he would be losing his deer hunting with his buddies and fly fishing for trout in the clear, cold streams so near at hand. However, in Missouri he found delight in quail hunting. He was an excellent shot and often brought home those delicacies for the family to enjoy.

Our lifestyle remained simple, but with a population of over 35,000, Joplin was certainly a different place than Washburn. Joplin was a small city. There were busses and street cars and buildings nine stories tall that required elevators! We settled into a modest house in a middle-class neighborhood and began to make new friends. We did have more opportunities—better schools, the use of the private swimming pool at the plant, a church with an organ and three or four real movie theaters.

Five years later the Depression settled upon the nation. I noticed little change in my life. Daddy continued going to work every day even though the plant was running less than half the time. We were in high school by now, and, like teenagers anywhere, blissfully unaware of the troubles of the wider world. We had no idea how lucky we were.

Blossom and I, two years apart, had always been close. Being the youngest of four we were always referred to as "the little girls". We shared a bedroom with twin beds and often when daddy got up in the morning and peeked into our room, we were both in the same bed.

Blossom was petite, just a little over 5'1", she had light brown hair, a small straight nose and she looked younger than her age. Conservative, a saver of everything, she was especially good with money. In her dresser drawers at home she had little boxes, one filled with pennies, one with nickels, one with dimes. Since we both had wonderful "stuff" we often had 'trade day.' Each of us would lay out on the bed everything we wanted to trade and we would swap. Most of the time she got the best of the deal.

She was always mindful of getting our mother's approval. I was more venturesome. When we made dresses, we would lay our fabric out on the dining table and pin on the patterns. Invariably I would start to cut and Blossom would worry, "Did Mother say?" No, but I wanted to do it anyway and quite often I had to buy a little more fabric because I didn't have the pattern placed right. So, being not too much alike, we got along beautifully.

It was not always sisterly sweetness and light. Blossom also had a bit of a temper. Sometimes, when we were growing up, doing dishes in the kitchen, if something made her angry, she would hurl things. A spatula or small pan. Mother would come out and settle her down with a few words. This throwing habit left her as she matured, though she still needed to vent her anger somehow. While we were in Italy, if she got mad, she would say "I'm taking the next boat home!" and storm out of the room. She always cooled off after a time and became again my loving sister with a bright sense of humor and a sparkling personality.

The most memorable thing about the Depression were the men that came to the back door in the evening asking for food. These men were traveling from place to place trying to find work. Blossom and I were usually in the kitchen doing dishes when we would hear a knock at the back-porch screen door. They were such a variety of ages, dress and demeanor, but always hungry. Fixing a plate for them, using our dishes and silver, developed in us a feeling of compassion. If the man happened to be young and handsome, we gave him extra goodies. Sometimes they asked if they could do anything for us and occasionally, we had them sweep the walk. One time it was early, only about 4 o'clock (my father was just coming home from work) when a man asked if dad had an extra hat. Daddy took the one off his head and gave it to him.

My mother and father used their money well. We had good meals in the evening around the dining table. Saturday night was hamburger night and it was a treat when we bought them at a hamburger stand, for a nickel, instead of making them at home. Grills and outdoor cooking had not taken over then. With our hamburgers we had potato chips and that was the only time we had chips. They were not a snack.

My parents spent their money on our college education. Harriet went to Missouri University. and Dick went to Michigan and Arkansas. Blossom went to Arkansas for four years and I spent two years in a local community college and taught a kindergarten class in the family basement. We watched our elder siblings earning degrees and beginning successful lives — we were always told, "Your time is coming."

I have a photograph dated April 30, 1917—nineteen days after I was born. It shows my whole family—now that I am there, our family is whole and complete—for the first time. We are seated on the steps of a porch. The wood looks new and freshly painted which is to be expected in a newly built mining town in Montana. It must be Sunday, and a warm, sunny one—a pleasant novelty for April in the Northern Rockies, I expect. Everyone is dressed up. My father, young and slim and dark-haired, wears a celluloid collar and broad necktie, and holds a cheroot in his teeth. In celebration, no doubt, of my arrival.

The Fahrig Family April 30, 1917

I am on my mother's lap, of course, supported by the crook of her arm. She is dressed in her best dress, dark with horizontal stripes, long sleeved, floor length, the cloth still looking crisp and shiny. Her hair is pulled back in a bun—as always, a bit the Victorian schoolmarm— though her collar is open to the welcome sunlight. She is looking down at my long white gown, her hand protectively on my chest. My sister Blossom is huddled beside my mother, my brother Dick is next to my father with a pennywhistle in his hands. We five are all seated on the top step. Only my sister Harriet, age 8, is looking at the camera from her seat on a lower step between my parent's feet. Her hands are clasped in her lap and she smiles forthrightly as though to proclaim her independence, already, from the family behind her.

There is something telling in this casual portrait. Harriet would indeed take her own step out into the world. Fourteen years after this photo was taken, she went to Italy and married an Italian.

Mother went to Italy in 1935 to be with Harriet when she had Dickie, her first child. Mother stayed several months and loved the whole experience. It must have been then that the idea was born to have Blossom and me spend time with Harriet and Franco and feel the magic of Italy. Mother, in her wisdom, felt the best sort of education would be to let us travel. Looking back now, I think they probably started setting money aside for just that purpose.

By 1938, after Blossom had finished four years at the University of Arkansas, while I had two years of college at a small school in nearby Pittsburg, Kansas.

It was our turn at last.

Americanata

Blossom waves as we leave Joplin, January 19, 1938

The Journey Begins

In 1938 I was twenty and my sister Blossom twenty-two. Our parents thought it would be a good use of their savings to have us spend a year in Milan with our sister Harriet. Our mother had visited Harriet only three years before and had a clear grasp of the expenses we would incur. Father, after more than thirty years working as a maintenance supervisor for various du Pont dynamite factories, felt secure with his employment. They had conferred together and with mutual respect, had decided this journey was within their means. Looking back now, it does seem a remarkable decision to send the two of us to Europe during the Great Depression!

It also speaks to the confidence they had in each other. She trusted in his steady ability as a breadwinner and wise leader on the dangerous factory floor where explosives were handled. (One legend of his tough integrity was the story of his firing a man he knew and liked for coming to work with a single wooden match in his pocket.)

And he trusted and respected mother's judgement. This trip was her idea, and she worked with her usual flair and imagination to anticipate every eventuality. Most importantly, our mother had excellent networking and leadership skills. She had built close friendships among the leading families (especially with the wives) who cycled through the Midwest on du Pont business. She was also a lifetime member of the Daughters of the American Revolution and rose to a position of influence in that conservative organization. Certainly, Florence Short Fahrig gave her daughters a powerful model of imaginative planning and capability to emulate.

She had worked hard imagining and organizing every step of the trip we were about to take on both sides of the Atlantic. There were four bon voyage parties and many going away gifts which added to the exhilaration. The gifts included hankies, toilet articles, silk stockings (in a new red shade), and a small packet with tiny clothes pins and clothesline. We took scads of clothes, filling nine suitcases and two trunks. Each of us had a knitting bag and a purse, as well. In 1938, a time before nylon and clothes dryers, we did not think "travel light."

We knew it would be difficult to find American silk stockings in Italy, and we wanted to take some to Harriet, so we packed 36 pairs. It sounds ridiculous now, but remember, silk doesn't wear like nylon or rayon or these wonderful modern fibers. It amazes me to think that our mother did not object when we wanted to take our riding boots. Not that we intended to ride horses, but jodhpurs and riding boots were a big fashion item then, so we packed them. I wonder now if she wasn't fulfilling some hidden Hollywood fantasy of her own as she packed her daughters off with these lovely costumes.

At that time American foods were not available in Italy and Harriet longed for tastes from home. Up from the basement my father brought an old steamer trunk, which we filled with goodies: brown sugar, cranberries, Jell-O, and pecans. Word of our trip spread through the community and when the Junge Baking Company in Joplin heard that Harriet wanted crackers and cookies, they brought us a huge box of these crispy treats. The pecans, still in the shells of course, we stuffed into the riding boots and they fit very nicely in the steamer trunk.

My father wanted to be sure the old steamer would hold together so he wrapped it tightly with heavy rope. As I looked at that ratty trunk, I had a mental picture of it being hoisted out of the ship's hold. What if they dropped it and it burst open spilling all that food onto the dock? As I watched Dad tie the knots in the rope I told him of my concern, I'd be so embarrassed!! In his dear understanding way, he leaned back on his haunches and said, "Honey, if that happens, just say 'tsk, tsk,' and walk away."

We were to leave in January and sail on the Italian liner The Vulcania, but lots of planning was needed to get us to New York. It so happened that one of the first of the fast new 'Super Trains,' The Green Diamond, had just been introduced, running from St. Louis to Chicago. These were not the old-fashioned black steam engines which clickety-clacked along the track, burning coal and filling the passengers' eyes with great clouds of sooty smoke. No, these new high-speed trains were the first streamlined, diesel engines which could rip down the track at up to 100 miles an hour. They were shining steel, with sealed windows to keep them quiet and clean.

"Oh, couldn't we go on the new streamliner?" we pleaded with Dad and Mother. It was a little out of the way to go to Chicago, but it also happened to be a time when Blossom's bosses were to be in that city for the Furniture Mart. Blossom worked in the office of Newman's Furniture store and had a wonderful relationship with Mr. Newman and Mr. Morgenthaler, the manager, a wonderfully kind, fatherly type. Both of them were interested in our impending trip and said they would like very much to meet us in Chicago so they could show us the sights. They must have spoken to our parents, they were all friends anyway, because Father relented. His final comment on the matter was "Well, I'm just glad the Super Train isn't going to Denver."

Early in the evening of January 9th we had a terrific send-off. Fourteen of our friends and family, including my dear Grandmother Short, gathered at the station to say goodbye. They brought candied fruit, perfume, books, compacts, candy and all the best wishes in the world. This first leg of the journey would be on an older, steam driven train. It would take all night to reach St. Louis and our seats would convert to beds, an upper and lower berth. I felt an atmosphere of hushed elegance upon entering the Pullman car. We met a polite, smiling attendant, eager to help us feel comfortable in this long, massive, rolling hotel. There were only a few people. Their voices were quiet, muffled by the plush, dark green velour seats, which faced each other like pairs of small sofas down both sides of the long car. There were two double-pane windows between each set of seats and above them, folded against the ceiling and looking like a wide mahogany molding, were the upper berths.

Mother and dad had climbed into the Pullman car with us, took turns taking our hands in theirs and telling us they loved us and wishing us 'happy journey'—mother's eyes were dry but dad's were moist. They helped us settle in our assigned seats in the car then returned to the platform to wave with the others. I told Daddy that I'd look for the most interesting stamps for his collection.

He replied, "Use a couple to write me a letter or two!" and I promised I would. They went back and joined our friends on the platform to wave goodbye.

Blossom and I sat facing each other, our heads against the window-panes, to wave goodbye. Very slowly and silently we began to move away from the station. The smooth, almost elegant movement of the train was like the first step in a long and graceful waltz. As I watched my parents and friends receding through the window, my dear sister beside me, tears came to my eyes and a lump to my throat.

This was the first of many departures our journey would bring, but it was the most significant. I would not see Joplin nor Mother and Dad for over a year. The child that I had been missed them already. A year was beginning that would forever influence my life. As the train picked up speed and whirled us into the night, Blossom and I sat back and sighed. Then we tucked away the sadness of departure and began to unfold our enthusiasm as though it were a crisp new map of the world. We were away at last!

It was 6:15 p.m. and would take 11 hours to reach St. Louis. At seven o'clock, dinner was announced and we made our way to the dining car. It too, had an aura of elegance: white tablecloths, gleaming crystal and silver, fresh flowers on each table. This car was full and we were seated with an "older" woman – at least she seemed so to me, but she probably was only 45 or so. Dinner was a leisurely, wonderful meal. Railroad dining cars were noted for their delicious food.

By the time we got back, our car had been transformed. Our seats were now made up into bunk beds with heavy green curtains hanging at the aisle to give privacy. We took our suitcases to the ladies' room and changed into our pajamas. Sleep came to us quickly, lulled by the gentle sway of the train.

The steward awakened us early in St. Louis as we had requested, and we changed to the Super Green Diamond bound for Chicago. Changing was easy as we each carried one suitcase. The rest of our luggage was sent directly to Pier 92 in N.Y. to be put on the Vulcania.

Chicago

The day trip to Chicago was exciting, partly because we were traveling so fast. During lunch in the diner Blossom asked the waiter how fast we are going. He replied, "95 miles an hour." Imagine! We had never traveled so fast.

Mr. Newman and Mr. Morgenthaler were there to meet us when we arrived in Chicago at 2 p.m. Mr. Newman was a wonderful looking man, tall, black hair, chiseled features. He was part of the little theater in Joplin and had won our young hearts when we saw him in several productions. Mr. Morgenthaler was the manager of the furniture store where Blossom worked in the office—it was her first real job after college. A solid, fatherly man of great charm and kindness, he was the father of one of my classmates in high school. Meeting them like this in a strange city somehow changed our relationship, giving us all a feeling of excitement and seemed to diminish the difference in our ages.

They hailed a cab and I felt the new adventure of it for I had seldom ridden in a taxicab. This was the first large city we had ever been in and what a beauty it was. Lake Michigan, that beautiful blue, freshwater sister of the great Superior we knew as children—lapped at the very feet of Chicago. The city seemed to rise right up out of the lake like an apparition. The water was so blue, and the buildings so tall I couldn't get enough of it. The contrast of the lake against the city made my heart pound. The endless, blue vacancy of nature meeting the massive confines of the grey stone skyscrapers sweeping gracefully along the shore—I had never seen anything like it.

The first stop was our hotel, The Palmer House, to freshen up and check in. Then to the huge Merchandise Mart, owned by the Kennedys, who meant nothing to me. In 1938 how could we know that in our lifetime the whole world would come to know the Kennedy family.

After seeing the sights of the city, these dear men took us shopping the at the famous Marshall Field's department store. We had heard of this store over and over as we listened to the radio to hear the Ben Bernie or Wayne King orchestras with that wonderful big band sound coming from the Trianon Ballroom in Chicago. Listening to these and other bands and their singers was one way that Blossom and I were able to learn the words of all the popular songs. Blossom was good at short-hand and having learned the words we would sing along with this lovely music. We harmonized—Blossom's sweet, high voice taking the melody while I sang the alto. It was a great time for music and it's gratifying to hear some of those wonderful songs still being played and sung on the radio. It was also music we loved to dance to and, like most young people our age, we were good at it.

We had dinner in the Empire Room of the Palmer House, which was one of Chicago's best hotels. It thrilled us with its elegance. Even the sil-verware on the table for instance, was heavier than we were used to, and in the room the large white towels, were thick, soft, and monogrammed. Nothing was lost on us. We were joined by a Mr. and Mrs. Sorby for dinner. Mr. Newman asked us what we would like and then ordered for us. This was a first for us and made us feel pampered and thoroughly part of the 'grown-up' world. After we had finished our meal, a time of hovering waiters, toasts with wine and happy conversation, I sat back with a happy sigh.

Then, Mr. Morgenthaler asked, "What would you think about going dancing?"

"We would love it!" Blossom and I said in unison. I think it was then that we knew in our hearts that our policy on this trip would be to let no opportunity pass to have fun.

"Great. We want to show you the Chez Paree."

So on to that famous night club where we danced to the music of Henry Bussie's orchestra. How we loved that. These charming men were wonderful dancers and made us feel very special indeed. I thought of the last time I'd danced in our high school gymnasium with the other kids, and it made me realize that I had now stepped across an important line. Tonight, for the first time I saw myself as a woman in a mature society of other men and women. I belonged here! I felt lucky to have had such a sweet initiation, and grateful to these kind men who were our escorts. They were both handsome with impeccable manners, plenty of resources and they seemed delighted to squire us around. Although we didn't think about it, they were probably having as good a time as we were.

It was a perfect day and evening, which lasted until the wee small hours. When they delivered us to our hotel room, our age difference returned, an appropriate gulf opening between us. We thanked them, said goodnight, and went to bed.

Washington, DC

We departed Chicago on a high note. This trip was going very well, in fact beyond our dreams. Mr. Newman insisted on paying for our hotel and even thanked us for coming. He took us to the train. It was 10 a.m., January 11th, and we were on our way to our nation's capital. It would take twenty hours on another older train, giving us another night on a Pullman starting at Youngstown, Ohio (I might add here that the cost of the Pullman for one night was $2.50).

Mother had planned this trip for us and contacted many old friends from the du Pont plant in Washburn, Wisconsin. As well as some who became good friends in the younger days building that factory together in Montana which supported the copper mining so important during the war in France. (They brought me into the world along with that dynamite plant!)

Through the years as people were transferred around, (the company did that a lot), they all became good friends and kept in close touch with each other. As we traveled east, we would be entertained and looked after by these old family friends, many of whom had prospered. It's important to remember that these friends who took such good care of us on this trip were much wealthier than we. They were executives in du Pont and some lived in mansions. We were the daughters of a factory worker. Yes, daddy was a supervisor, a boss on the factory floor and well liked, but there was a distinct difference between us. Our close relationship to them was the trump card in our wise mother's hand in planning this trip.

Arriving in Washington at 6:30 in the morning, we checked into the Lee Hotel, even though we were to visit in the home of our parents' good friends, the Alvords. This way we got a little more sleep and bathed before the Alvords' chauffeur, Johnson, picked us up at 11 a.m. It seems extravagant to think that we checked into a hotel room for only four and a half hours, but that is what we did! Mother had been concerned that we not disturb the Alvords at the unseemly hour of six a.m.

To see Washington for the first time was an experience so profound we could hardly believe we were there. The chauffeur took us to the Alvords large house on the outskirts of the city. The Alvords were good friends of my folks from years they shared in Washburn, Wisconsin. Mr. Alvord was now a tax expert to whom Congress often looked for advice. Mrs. Alvord, a motherly sort, stayed home while her daughter, (who was considerably older than we) and Johnson, their chauffeur, made sure we saw the most important places. My favorite was the Lincoln Memorial. He was always my favorite president and the simple, gracious design of the building suited him to a tee. The weather was nippy, but we were comfortable as we drove around in their big town car. As we passed the White House, Johnson told us the Roosevelts were in Warm Springs, Ga.

The Alvords' home was lovely and inviting. We had dinner there and afterward visited until bedtime. Usually at home we would take our time getting to bed, often going to the kitchen to get a bite to eat. But here, within minutes everyone was in their bedroom and the house was dark. The upstairs hall was square and our bedroom was near the stairs. We put on our PJ's and together went into the bathroom which was at the far side of the hall. Blossom finished washing and pinning up a few curls in her hair and went back to the bedroom. When I was ready, I shut off the light, opened the door and found myself in the pitch-black hall. Cautiously feeling my way along and trying to avoid a table that was close to our doorway, I moved to my left and suddenly found myself flying through the air and down the stairs. My slippers, with little wooden heels came off and clattered down each step. I lay on the landing and in the silence that followed all this noise, I heard Blossom tittering. I fumbled around for my slippers, got up and was grateful to find I was not hurt. Back in our room Blossom and I got the giggles but we tried not to be heard.

The next morning at Breakfast Mrs. Alvord said, "I thought I heard someone fall last night and was afraid you might be hurt, but then I heard you laugh and I knew you were all right."

I thought to myself, "I could have broken a leg and lain there all night just because Blossom laughed."

That morning another friend, Mrs. Hudson, picked us up and took us to see Mount Vernon. What a thrill to see Washington's estate. Being able to walk around it, seeing the rear entrance, which never shows in the pictures, gave us a feeling of what it was to live in that long ago time. Mrs. Hudson took us to the train to Wilmington where we were to visit the Evans. More friends my parents made through the du Pont Co.

The rest of our time in the east was a whirl of visits and stay-overs with du Pont friends. There was Mrs. Hudson, the Evans for three days, the Welfords, and the Axelburgs, all of whom were gracious and kind. They showed us all the points of interest including Longwood, the gardens of Pierre du Pont. That was a showplace indeed, and best of all, Mr. and Mrs. du Pont were there directing preparations for a huge party. There were dozens of large round tables with pink cloths draped to the floor. Tall five-socket candelabra, with large bunches of grapes hanging from them, graced the center of each table. I was so impressed.

There were dinners, bridge parties, dances, and dates. Often, we were up and out 'til the early hours of the morning. One of the great blessings of youth which we depended on many times during this trip was the ability to party into the wee hours and recover the next day. Of course, we were living very "high on the hog" as the folks in Missouri would say. We had no jobs or obligations of any kind—we could sleep till noon if we wanted, and sometimes we did.

The last stop before New York was with the Axelburgs, who Blossom and I knew very well. They had lived in Joplin many years and had shared a number of holidays with our family. When we got to their house, a modest one with a great deal of warmth to it, I had the feeling of being home. We were all tired and Mrs. Axelburg came in to tuck us in bed and kiss us goodnight. Was this homesickness I felt?

We were now in Gibbstown, New Jersey and some time in these next few days we were with a group that included Jim Castner. Jim, a good friend of my brother Dick, had a marvelous job with the du Pont Co. He was a great guy, but in that first moment of meeting I could sense him looking me over as a romantic prospect. That caused me to instinctively take a step back. In my twenty-year-old eyes, he seemed too old. He must have been thirty-two or thirty-three. He told us that he would love to come to New York to see us off. Imagine! After all this high stepping, going, seeing, and still there was New York ahead of us!

New York City

On Jan 19th we stepped off the train in New York City and took a cab to the Taft Hotel. We had a quick lunch at the Horn and Hardhart Automat, something we had heard of and dreamed of doing for years. It was a place with a wall of little glass doors, behind which were various foods. You put a nickel in the slot and it opened the little glass door to get out your sandwich or pie or whatever. It was the first vending machine.

Then we went to the pier to see about our trunks and luggage. The Vulcania was there and we were fortunate enough to meet a man who represented the shipping line and showed us all around the boat. What a jewel! We would be on it for two weeks as this sailing took a cruise around the Mediterranean. The most important thing we found out was that she sailed at midnight Thursday instead of Friday noon as we had thought.

When we got back to our hotel room, we found mail from home and several messages from friends. Mrs. Burk would see us the next day, Mr. and Mrs. Johnston asked us to go to dinner that evening and would call for us at the hotel.

We had an errand to do for one of Harriet's friends in Italy. Her name was Sophia Gallo. Her husband, Fortune Gallo, a well-known impresario, had a package we were to pick up at his New York office and take to his wife. We had the address which, when we looked on the map, was just a few blocks over and several blocks down from our hotel. Blossom was tired so I said I would go. It gave me a thrill to go out in that fabulous city and find my way. I had no trouble finding the right building, took the elevator and entered the office of Fortune Gallo. No one paid the slightest attention to me.

After waiting a few minutes, I finally said, "May I see Mr. Gallo?"

A woman working at what I took to be a reception desk answered, "Mr. Gallo is not in." I stood for a moment feeling foolish as she went back to her papers, "Excuse me," I finally said, "but I am to pick up a package from him to take to his wife in Italy." There was an immediate transformation as she stood up with a beaming smile." Oh, you are Miss Fahrig? Yes, we have been expecting you. Do sit down and I will get the package."

Two other girls came out to say hello and to send greetings to Mrs. Gallo. When the package appeared, I was a little taken aback. I had expected something the size of a shoe box. This was more like a very large suit box. I managed to get it back to the hotel where we read the note on the outside, telling customs what was inside. Among other things listed were "Two Pairs of Adult Size Dr. Denton Footed Pajamas."

The Johnstons picked us up at 6:30 and took us to the newest event on Broadway. It was Billy Rose's Casa Manana, a theater-restaurant with a comedy review called Lets Play Fair. Talk about a wonderful evening. In the first place, the Johnstons were such fun—they made us feel that we were as much fun for them as they were for us. Mrs. Johnston made a particularly strong impression on me. She had such poise and self-assurance on the telephone—I remember thinking that I wanted to be like her.

At the beginning of this journey Mother told us "Travel is the great educator. Yes, you'll see many new places, and gain a new appreciation for the size and variety of the great wide world; but most importantly, you'll meet many new people, and each one will be an opportunity to learn something new. You'll come back having made decisions about who you are and how you want to behave. That's the task of the young, to become a person of the world."

As we learned about the great city of New York that day, one of the centers of that world mother had spoken of, Mrs. Johnston seemed the perfect guide, I could almost hear Florence Fahrig in far away Joplin whisper in my ear—"Pay attention!"

That evening under the elegant, fretted ceiling of a Broadway theatre, Blossom and I were simply enchanted. We had a wonderful table in the center and quite close to the large proscenium. The food was delicious. I was so torn between watching the show and eating, that when I looked down once they had removed my plate and I wasn't finished. However, there was more coming, wine and dessert. We couldn't thank the Johnstons enough and they made us promise to call them when we returned. I kept the program from the evening and note now that the cost for this extravaganza was $2.50 apiece, first three tiers 50 cents extra.

The next morning a telegram arrived from Jim Castner. "Arriving noon wait lunch for me." Well, we didn't even get dressed till noon. Then we met Jim, who had also taken a room at the Taft, for lunch. By this time, we had acclimated ourselves to the pace of the city and were infected with its giddy energy. Over lunch with Jim we planned our day and evening in New York. For the afternoon, Mrs. Burk, yet another friend of Mother's, caught up with us and drove us all around to get an overall view of the city.

My lasting impression of seeing this wondrous city for the first time was of miles and miles of tall buildings. We drove for more than half an hour and never got out of the canyons of those big structures on each side. It was a jolt to realize that the entire population of Joplin could occupy a single building. "Like cliff dwellings," I thought, looking at the apartments and hotels stacked up on every side. Mrs. Burk was a delight and between her and Jim we had an afternoon of new sights, learning, laughter and awe. She dropped us back at the Taft a little before five, and we all thanked her for the wonderful gift she had given us.

We had to check out of our room by 5 o'clock, so we moved over to Jim's room to dress for dinner. Jim had brought us a gift of a very large, lightweight suitcase—telling us we would need it to bring lots of things home from Italy. What a great gift! So thoughtful of him, and we would indeed fill it for our return.

For our last evening in New York, we dressed in our best. We had each tucked in a long dress just in case. Never be caught short. Jim looked good in spite of his mustache, which made him look even older, but he was very sophisticated. I by contrast, felt naive and somewhat uncomfortable when Jim and I were alone while Blossom was dressing in the bathroom. I had never been alone in a hotel room with a man before and for some reason couldn't find anything to say. Apparently neither did he. When we were ready, we admired one another and declared ourselves ready for the best New York could throw at us.

We took a cab uptown to Rockefeller Center. There, forty stories above Manhattan was the fabled Rainbow Room, one of the pinnacles of smart society. Radio programs originated there that Blossom and I had listened to countless times. We would lie on the carpet in our living room in Joplin imagining ourselves there, beautifully dressed, escorted by handsome men, dancing and dining above the glittering lights of the greatest city in the world. Now, we found the reality surpassed our dreams. When the elevator reached the top, the doors opened and a thrilling surge of music lifted us like a wave and carried us into a shining world of beautiful people and glittering surfaces. There was the happy clatter of flatware on china and the tinkle of ice in cocktail glasses. Through the windows on every side the lights of the city spread out beneath us like gems on black velvet, glistening far into the clear winter night. Everywhere people laughed and drank and danced to the massed saxophones on the bandstand. Blossom and I dove in and played like children in the surf, savoring each moment of our last evening in America.

It all ended in a crowded taxi to the pier; we, our luggage and dear Jim so helpful at every turn. He took us up the gangplank and saw us to our stateroom which was filled with flowers, gifts and 40 letters and telegrams — to think we had so many and such loving friends! Then Jim got off and stood on the pier and we stood at the rail and waved to him. Suddenly I noticed the space between the ship and the pier began to widen. Just at that moment the ship's horn sent out a blast that was so loud it brought tears to my eyes. I found myself trembling with excitement. All our journey of the past ten days had been to bring us to this moment. This was the ultimate leave-taking, departing from our homeland. The skyline of New York ablaze with lights, Jim at the rail throwing kisses, the horn so loud and piercing, the stately motion of the ship...it was a moment that would never leave me.

The Voyage

The Vulcania

This ship would be our home for two weeks. We would cross the Atlantic, cruise the western Mediterranean, and finally disembark at Genoa. Sailing at midnight, as we did, left no time to unpack before we fell into bed. We did read a few of our many letters and the telegrams. The next morning there was much to do. The cabin was quite comfortable with a nice little bath. We unpacked what we thought we would need, keeping some things in the suitcases, but several suitcases and the two trunks were down in the hold.

Life aboard an ocean liner is unlike life anywhere else. First of all, you discover the meaning of the phrase "getting your sea legs." The winter Atlantic for the first few days of the voyage was quite choppy and the action of the ship was unsteady to say the least. Sometimes the vessel rolled from side to side, other times it pitched front to back — which made you a good deal less steady on your feet. Blossom was more affected by the movements than I, and during the voyage she spent a couple of days in bed. For me, the worst part was being closed in. Bathrooms got me. When standing in front of the sink I would feel myself suddenly toppling backwards – I would lurch and hang on for dear life. The towels would be hanging straight out from the wall. I found it so unsettling that I would hurry up to the deck for air. The trick I found was to try to focus on the ship itself and ignore the horizon.

Of the three classes, first, tourist, and steerage, we were happy with our lot — tourist. We soon learned that first class was mostly older couples with, I am sure, lots of money. Our class had younger folks. There were two other young ladies, and best of all, four single men. We spent the first day familiarizing ourselves with the ship and its decks. The Vulcania was not a large ship. In fact, by the standards of the great ocean liners, she was tiny. In place of the four great smokestacks of the Titanic or the Lusitania, she had only a single one. There could not have been more than two hundred of us passengers aboard in all three classes, probably fewer. Still, to us she was a mighty vessel and we were pleased as any admirals to be crossing the Atlantic in so grand a fashion. The Italian officers and staff kept the ship in spotless condition.

The air was still chilly, though, and the water choppy, so our deck chairs got little use.

At dinner we met people. The dining room was the full width of the boat with windows on both sides. Ships were always characterized as "floating palaces," and it was in the public spaces that the designers tried to live up to the appellation. The dining rooms, ballrooms, grand staircases and promenades were lavishly appointed. There was no end of brass and mahogany, crystal chandeliers and plush carpeting. Our dining room was filled with tables of various sizes, each covered with spotless linen and crisp white napkins. The waiting staff was masculine and Italian, so Blossom and I, being the only unescorted women, got perhaps more than our share of their attention.

We were assigned to a table of eight and we liked the people with whom we were seated. I loved sitting at that table, looking at the large menu and knowing I could order anything I wanted. It was already paid for! The first evening I started off with soup — a broth with rice — and the waiter came and asked if I cared for cheese. I looked at what he was holding in his hand and it was a glass dish with a silver lid on a hinge, and a spoon. He pressed a lever and bingo! A spoonful of grated cheese. I wondered where he would put it. Figuring the way to find out was to say, "Yes, please," I watched as he sprinkled it over my soup! Imagine!! It tasted divine. I looked at Blossom and we both smiled. We were enjoying this.

Seated at our table were two young men with whom we would share wonderful times on this trip. They were Mack Herman and Paolo Beccaria. Paolo was Italian, about twenty-five, tall and graceful. He had a dark complexion and a dazzling smile, was always impeccably dressed and spoke no English. He would be the first man who ever kissed my hand in an earnest, courtly way — not the jokey fashion one's older brother adopts. He was so charming and eager to visit that I found myself learning Italian in order to know him better. This involved a good deal of playing charades to communicate. It turned out that he was a doctor, a recent graduate, apparently, from medical school. Mack Herman, the other single man at our table, was American — from a small town in the mid-west. He was a sweet-natured boy-next-door sort, with a pudgy nose and thin, brown hair. I guessed he was twenty-six years old, taking his first trip to "the continent." It always amused me that Europe was referred to as "the continent," as though it were the only one.

After dinner that first evening, we saw a movie —The Fleet's In. Then we went to the ballroom. This was a magnificent room— again, the width of the ship—and with a doubly high ceiling using the full height of two decks. You entered from the dining room down a sweeping stairway from a promenade that circled the dance floor on the deck above. There was a large crystal chandelier in the center and a bandstand with a twelve- or fifteen-piece orchestra playing all the latest hits. We were in 'hog heaven' and we might have said so if we hadn't felt the necessity to keep our language as swanky and sophisticated as the surroundings.

Happily, there were plenty of good dance partners, and we made lots of new friends. Frank Hutton was one young man we met that night.

Frank, eighteen or nineteen, was tall, handsome, and very quiet. He explained that his mother did almost all the talking to their dinner table and so he wasn't very good at it. There was the air of an aristocrat about him, an aloofness and reserve that seemed mature in one so young. He was taking a break from studies at Yale.

We also met another mid-westerner, Larry Quip, from Indiana. Larry was a bright, steady sort who was easy to talk to and made me feel comfortable at once. We danced well together, and at one point, while discussing our names, I mentioned that my middle name was Ann, but nobody ever called me that.

"Would you like me to?" Larry offered.

"Yes, call me Ann." It suited me to have another identity, this experience was so unlike anything that Becky Fahrig had ever experienced before. To be dancing in a marvelous ballroom in a floating palace on the Atlantic Ocean on my way to "The Continent!" I was 'Ann' at last. Take my picture, someone!

The next day was Saturday, January 22nd, and we had breakfast in bed. It was a rough sea and Blossom felt sick so she just stayed in bed. I sat up on the deck most of the afternoon getting more acquainted with Paul, Larry, Mack, Gladys and a Dr. Carpenter. In the evening there was a party and I felt so badly that Blossom still felt ill. There were games and 'horse races.' I won second prize which was a badge of three colored ribbons. The purser pinned them on me and we then sat and visited. The purser is the ship's officer in charge of the passengers. He was an Italian named Emilio who spoke good English and wore wonderful smelling after shave. He seemed nice, but a flirt.

Sunday, January 23rd, was very windy and rolling. Blossom was still sick and even I lost it over the railing once. That night the purser asked me to sit at his table, apparently a big honor. There were just the two of us. The sea was so rough that evening that the orchestra had to leave the dance. Most of us felt queasy as well, so we all went to bed early. Everyone teased me about the purser.

We slept late the next morning and woke to find a beautiful, warm and sunny day. Blossom felt fine at last, and we spent the afternoon on deck G playing shuffleboard and taking pictures. At 3:30 they rolled out a large tea cart and served us hot bullion, crispy breads and huge green stuffed olives. We were joined by a man named Parker Cushing from first class. He said we had the life. He said first class was quiet and dull and he envied us with our laughter and singing and having so much fun.

Late that evening just before bedtime, a group of us were talking in the smoking room when we heard shouts and someone rushed in and said, "Come look." We all went out on deck where lots of others were gathered at the port railing. Looking north the sky was ablaze with red.

"What is it?"

"Another ship on fire?"

"But it's way too big for that."

"This is Tuesday and Thursday we will be at Madeira Island, so what land would be north of us?"

Someone said it looked like the whole city of London was on fire. It had streaks of white and went high into the sky. The next morning, we learned it was the aurora borealis giving all of Europe a big show.

First Landfall

T hursday morning, the 27th, we woke at six and saw land looming in the distance, and what beautiful land it was. The Madeira Islands are higher than I had imagined and wonderfully green. We dressed and went on deck to watch our approach. The steamship company provided a little brochure guide for us passengers. Here is what I learned about Madeira:

These islands were known to the ancient Romans but were not inhabited until early in the fifteenth century when the Portuguese rediscovered them and settled there. The Portuguese still own the islands, two of which are inhabited. The word "Madeira" means 'wood' in Portuguese, and when the islands were first discovered they were thickly wooded. The Portuguese cleared the land by lighting fires that burned for seven years. The ash left from these fires fertilized the soil and made it ideal for growing grapes. The wise Portuguese brought grapevines from Cyprus and planted sugar cane from Sicily to provide for a self-sufficient wine-making industry on the island. Hence the famous wine which carries the archipelago's name.

The islands were a glorious sight as we approached from the west at dawn. After a week of unbroken views of the Atlantic, to come now to these lovely bits of earth, their mountaintops shrouded in a pink and golden mist, was enough to make me weep. The mist would burn away soon as the wind off the Sahara Desert, 400 miles beyond the horizon, brought us a tropical day. We could scarcely believe we had left a chilly January in New York only a week before.

We anchored in the harbor of the capitol city of Funchal — there was no dock big enough for the Vulcania. By 8:30 we were in the tender headed for land. The city was lovely with clean white buildings built on ground that rose steadily and sometimes steeply from the water. The foliage was lush and tropical and the gardens around the houses filled with unusual and beautiful flowers. Christopher Columbus lived on these islands for a time and married the daughter of the governor.

Paolo, Mack, Blossom and I decided to join forces to sightsee together this exciting day. We walked along narrow streets, climbing up away from the harbor. At last a bus came along and we took it to the crest of the nearest hill. We looked back to the ship far below us, sitting so majestically it seemed like a jewel in the blue, blue sea. By now the Vulcania had become our home and it gave me a feeling like the 'pride of ownership' to see her shining in the water.

We stayed at the top of the hill for an hour or so, walking around among the houses and gardens there. Everything was strange and new to Blossom and me — the red tile roofs on the clean, whitewashed houses, the curious foliage and unfamiliar birds, the sparkling tropical sky — it was our first taste of the world beyond our own country, and the experience made me feel wiser somehow, as I had when tasting champagne for the first time.

We took a bus down to the town itself and were suddenly besieged by little children begging for money. This was another first for us and I wanted to give them something, but the boys with us, as well as some of the friendly natives, told us if we did, we would soon become over-whelmed by hordes of demanding children. With sad faces, we closed our purses and the disappointed children soon lost interest in us and returned to their play.

Blossom and I wanted to see the workers embroidering the famous Madeira napkins. We were directed to a certain part of town and there we found young girls, some as young as eleven or twelve, working in the doorways of their houses or where the sunlight fell directly on their work. This fine needlework requires eyes that are sharp enough to dis-tinguish the exceedingly close weft of the linen, which is why the work must be done by girls so young. The needle must go into a certain hole between the threads to make the tiny, intricate patterns. As we grow older, our eyesight dims and adults find this precision impossible. It was touching to see these girls as they sat in the sunlight doing this won-derfully fine embroidery. Clearly there were no child labor laws here. When we went to the stores to buy the napkins they made, we found the price almost twice what they were in the states. Paolo said, "Tourist trap," and once more we closed our purses.

We had lunch in a funny little restaurant where the boys ordered wine. The wine list gave the age of the wines and the prices in dollars. A Madeira Bola up to 12 years old was 50 cents a bottle. Twenty-five-year-old wine was $1.00, and a 60-year-old bottle cost $5.00. We laughed and were having such a good time but the biggest laugh was when they brought the wine (one of the $1.00 ones) and Mack poured us each a drink. He looked at the bottle and there was a fly in it. This struck us as hilarious. The fly seemed considerably younger than twenty-five. We asked for another bottle and noticed that the waiter did not seem in the least perturbed by the fly. We wondered if a bug in the wine was a regular event? In any case, the wine was excellent.

In the afternoon we took a ride in a gayly decorated cart pulled by oxen. It was unusual because it was equipped with runners instead of wheels. It was only one of a batch of experiences that day that made us aware of the foreignness of the place. This was a feeling which would come over us time and again on our travels and provided one of the chief pleasures of the journey. To travel is to be forever discovering something new, and so to be forever re-defining the world. And of course, that was one of the things our parents had told us—that this trip would be educational, perhaps even the equivalent of college or university.

The tender was available anytime and as we didn't sail until midnight we went back to shore after dinner and went to what we all called a "joint". It was a waterfront dive with sailors and girls and funny concertina music — we four had a lot of fun. When we sailed at midnight, a group of divers came out as they had done in the morning when we arrived. If you threw coins into the sea they could dive and fetch them with amazing ease, even in the dark water. They came in swarms of small boats selling everything from bird cages to wicker chairs. Blossom regretted not buying napkins ashore and took advantage of these last-minute merchants to do so.

We had such a big day and didn't want to see it end, so after we sailed, we all had a party until the wee hours. By dawn we had at last exhausted our youthful energy. We collapsed and slept.

Friday was a blessed day at sea. Everyone was so tired from Madeira - the wine, the island and the party - that we rested all day in our staterooms. Tomorrow would find us in Casablanca and a new continent!

Africa

D awn came, bright and beautiful, and we were in Africa! What a difference from Madeira — or anyplace else I had ever been. Casablanca is on the north-western coast of Morocco facing the Atlantic Ocean — a large city where the desert meets the sea. It was made up of flat-roofed buildings with some domes and spires every so often to excite the eye. True to its name, the houses were all white. There was very little green, of course, and the air had a parched and dusty odor that interested the nose after so many days of fresh sea wind. I must say at once that the movie with Humphrey Bogart and Ingrid Bergman would not be made for many years yet. In fact, I had not yet become conscious of Bogart and before seeing the itinerary for this voyage, had not heard of the city of Casablanca. So, it was with eyes as fresh as any young Marco Polo's that I beheld this exotic, teeming place.

"Teeming" seems a particularly apt word to use here, as my first impressions of the people were of robed and dark-skinned crowds surging through the narrow streets. Sadly, my dominant impression of Casablanca is of poverty and squalor. Our ship was tied at the dock when we awoke that morning, and on the quay immediately in front of us were swarms of people. They had gathered beneath the gleaming paint and brass of our splendid ship to beg. Who could blame them for thinking us all Rockefellers? We strode excitedly down the gangplank to stand on their ground in our spotless clothes and white shoes, while they reached out from their coarse robes, "like gunny-sacks," as Blossom said. It was piteous and daunting — the more so since their numbers left us feeling as helpless as they.

We went ashore at 9 a.m. Mack, Paolo, and we again pooling our money and making up a foursome. We rented a taxi and a driver for the day at two dollars apiece. First, we drove to Rabat, the capital city of Morocco about 50 miles up the coast. The country, a barren, stony desert with now and then a palm tree or two, was a bit disappointing. I wanted the clean, sandy Sahara of the movies, with sheiks and camels, Legionnaires and Valentino. We passed a long procession of people walking at the side of the road. Some of them were wailing and crying loudly. It was a funeral procession and our guide told us the wailers had been hired as was the custom with burials in these parts.

Morocco was a French Protectorate in 1938 (it would gain independence in 1956). This land and these people reached their pinnacle in history during the tenth to thirteenth century. These were the Moors who conquered and occupied Spain in those years, bringing, among other things, mathematics and an elaborate architecture to Europe. We saw some of the architecture on display at the Sultan's Palace in Rabat.

Here were the distinctive archways, some keyhole shaped, others coming to a peak, like a gothic arch. But the most impressive thing about the building was the intricate stone filigree on the facade. What a great labor it must have taken to carve that amazingly precise geometric pattern. Islam, the religion of Morocco, forbids the depiction of any living thing in the graphic arts. The artists of Arab countries compensate for this proscription by creating wildly elaborate geometric patterns in stone, wood and ceramic tile. If you gaze at this art closely for a little while, it can have a hypnotizing, dizzying effect.

Rabat was a walled city, richer than Casablanca it seemed to us, with more foliage — gardens and a few large trees. Some of these trees were 'cork oaks' and were the remnants of a large forest that covered this area in ancient times. Most of the gardens were hidden from our view in private courtyards. Of course, we had to content ourselves with a view of the Sultan's Palace and the wall around his 'har-eem' from the street. We visited a museum of ancient artifacts and saw relics left by the Romans, Carthaginians, Vandals and Arabs who had claimed the land before the French.

We drove through the streets of the native quarters which was depressing. Here, too, the poverty was everywhere. The people wore brown sackcloth that completely covered them including their heads. A few were lying asleep against a building as if they had been tossed there.

We drove back to Casablanca and our guide said we must see a place where 500 girls live in a sort of walled compound which they never leave. We couldn't imagine such a thing. Were they held prisoner? But the guide said no, they choose to be there. The guide led us through halls and into a room with some straight chairs a low table and one window. He obviously had done this many times before. Some official came in and he and the guide had a discussion which of course we could not understand.

They seated us in the chairs. Blossom and I had not an idea in the world what was coming. In just a minute two young girls came in. They were lovely looking girls, wearing loose, flowing robes. The guide spoke to them and they took off their robes and stood before us naked. My first feeling was pity for them. They had such lovely bronze skin, beautifully shaped bodies and didn't seem to mind in the least that they were on display. I heard Blossom mutter "Oh jees". The guide kept talking to the girls as they stood there and then in some way they attached tassels to their breasts. To my utter surprise each girl started to move her muscles which caused the tassels to swing around in a rhythmic pattern. I was bug-eyed and embarrassed and didn't dare look at the boys we were with. All the time the guide was talking and sort of egging them on.

Mack, Paul (as we called him) Blossom and I had an arrangement to make up a kitty for times when we went ashore and one of the boys would pay the bills during the day. I found out later that we had paid extra to see these girls and I hope they got a benefit from it. As to whether I got my money's worth I guess I did, for I certainly learned something that I never thought existed. I learned also when embarrassed not to make a fuss but try to be poised and keep quiet.

I look back on that whole sorry incident with embarrassment for my own immaturity and cowardice. Why was I not angry? It was rude and thoughtless of those boys to subject us to such a show - as though we too, could get sexually excited by it. I think now of the true grown men we had danced with in Chicago who had the taste and maturity to respect us and would never have put us in such a shameful situation!

We sailed at eight that night from our first port in Africa, and because most of us were tired we danced only a little while before retiring. Tomorrow would be Gibraltar.

Gibraltar

Gibraltar was fascinating. I had always imagined it, from the famous pictures I had seen, as the last great mountain at the southernmost tip of Spain — the point closest to Africa. But it is actually many miles to the east of there, on the Mediterranean side of the narrow strait. "The Rock," as it is called by the people who live there, is well named, since it stands by itself on a long, narrow peninsula the rest of which is low, sandy ground. The whole place is only three miles long and 3/4 of a mile wide at the widest point. The Vulcania was moored in the harbor to the west of the Rock — off Gibraltar Bay, a deep, narrow body of water between the mainland and the peninsula.

This is one of the most fought-over pieces of ground in Europe. Though it is connected to Spain, the Spanish have controlled it for only about half the time in the past 2000 years. It was known to the Greeks as one of the Pillars of Hercules, the other being a Mountain in Morocco, across the straits of Gibraltar. The Moors conquered Spain in the year 711 led by one Tarik — his name is memorialized by the last syllable of Gibraltar. The Arab/Moorish name for the rock was Jubel al Tarik, ("Mountain of Tarik"), which time and translation have eroded into the word Gibraltar.

The Moors held on right up until 1492. While Columbus was discovering America, his patrons, Ferdinand and Isabella of Spain were driving the Moors out of Granada - their last foothold in Europe. Gibraltar is now a British Protectorate and has been a military base for the British since it was captured in 1704.

We woke to find the Vulcania riding at anchor in the harbor, which was filled with military ships of all sizes — gun boats, cruisers, naval ships from all over the world. We four teamed up again and took the tender in at 8:30 that morning. We rented a car and driver again to see as much as possible.

The town itself is quite small and hilly of course, being built on the rock. Driving as far North as possible, a matter of a mile and a half, we saw Spain across a barbed wire fence. There is a wide strip of land between Spanish and British territory that is known as "no man's land." As we looked across to Spain, we remembered that a terrible civil war was going on there. Many Spaniards had taken refuge in Gibraltar to save themselves from the violence in their country.

Our guide took us inside the rock through a complex maze of tunnels, some of them created by the Moors over a thousand years ago. We walked up long ramps through the limestone, occasionally finding holes looking out to sea. These were used as places for guns to defend the Rock. We climbed a long time, all the while the guide impressed on us the historical importance of this stony guardian at the entrance to the Mediterranean Sea.

One of the problems the defenders of the Rock faced was the absence of a steady water supply. Over the centuries they created a vast catchment basin and cistern. There is a huge smooth surface on the outside that catches the rainwater and drains it through pipes into enormous reservoir tanks carved deep in the heart of the Rock. They have a four-year supply of water stored. It is the largest such catchment system in the world.

When we started down, we all soon realized it was easier to climb than to descend. The slope was pretty steep and by the time we reached the bottom our legs and feet ached in spite of the comfortable sneakers we wore.

We sailed at 1 o'clock and spent the beautiful afternoon lolling in the sun. There was a small pool on deck. I dove in and was surprised to discover that it was salt water — a logical thing in retrospect, but another one of the little unexpected twists that kept these experiences fresh and pleasantly startling. It was pointed out that we were on about the same latitude as New York and while we basked in our bathing suits, folks on Fifth Avenue were still bundled up in winter coats. This was another curiosity and testament to the mighty Humboldt Current which brought the warmth of Florida and the Caribbean across the planet and saved western Europe from a chilly fate. But this is another of the many insights to come to me in retrospect. At the time of course, I was concerned only with the pleasures of the moment and the fun we were all having. We played shuffleboard and before dinner a large group gathered for a cocktail party.

A note on clothing is perhaps in order here. There were occasions when we would dress in our best on the ship — the men in dinner jackets or tuxedos, we girls in our long gowns and jewelry. Blossom and I had much smaller wardrobes than many of the women aboard, but with a few accessories, we managed to avoid looking like hicks. Most of the time we were in a more casual mode anyway. Men always wore jackets and ties to dinner, while we would wear one of our best dresses or a skirt and sweater combination. In 1938 no woman wore trousers of any kind. Silk stockings were de rigeur, with the attendant garter belt. It was about this time that Marlene Dietrich showed up in a film wearing pants and shocked the civilized world. World War II would change all this.

The evening went late and before going to bed I went to the upper deck to enjoy the night sky with Larry Quip, the sweet boy from Indiana who called me "Ann." It was a calm and balmy night, the stars lighting the tranquil sea. Larry and I talked about our dreams and plans for the future. It was romantic beyond anything I had yet experienced and I loved, not the boy so much as the moment. We talked a long time, and then he took me in his arms and kissed me. I felt like I was in a movie, and I wanted to play the part beautifully and well. It was so far from my ordinary everyday life back in Joplin that I could not give it serious credit. I think Larry was in the same frame of mind, good mid-westerner that he was. We stood there as much in Hollywood as the Mediterranean, each of us glad the other was there to partner us in the best love scene of our young lives. All in fun. Then we went to our separate staterooms.

Algiers

lgiers the next day. What a time we are having. This city has old and new in it and then of course the Casbah. That is the old mysterious part with narrow streets, more like little alleys winding through the maze of dirty stucco buildings. One could get lost in here so we stayed close to our guide. There are lots of steps in these narrow passages and filth was everywhere. Human excretion as well as animals. The Casbah was to be made famous by a movie that we would see later in Italy in which French actor Charles Boyer successfully hides in the Casbah from the police. "Come vith me to ze Casbah," was the line he made famous – uttering it with a throaty French accent under dark, hooded eyes. It may have been romantic in the movie, but my memories of the Casbah are only of the squalor and poverty. I was glad to get the heck out of there and back on the ship where the party was.

Bob Trotter, an Englishman, came aboard here. He was a vital and outgoing man in his 40's, I would guess; tall, dressed in a dark suit and spoke with a 'veddy' English accent. He conducted himself with great aplomb, introducing himself to us with ease and grace. We had a good time giving him a big welcome as he fit right in with our "gang."

The next day was Feb. 1st, and we spent the whole day at sea. Because it was another beautiful day we were out early and on deck most of the time. We all put our thinking caps on to come up with ideas for a costume for this night was the Masquerade Ball. I went as Cleopatra and Blossom was a Hula girl. I think the Purser found the grass skirt for her. He was still hovering around. It was so nice that everyone participated which made it a great success.

The next stop was Tripoli. We arrived at noon on the 2nd of February. It is also on the north shore of Africa, further east around the jut of land that is Algeria. Five of us this time went together in a horse-drawn cab to see the sights. It was a charming place and I liked it as much as anything we had seen so far. A good bit of it was modern. The Udaan Hotel was one of the most beautiful Hotels I had ever seen. We ate there and then played roulette and danced. We ended up in a little funny cafe for a nightcap and paid a dollar for five Brandies. Our ship dropped anchor there overnight so the next morning we went ashore again for a few hours to shop and send postcards before we said goodbye to Africa and sailed north at noon.

Friday the 4th having passed through the straits of Messina, between Sicily and Italy, we went on deck to see the Island of Stromboli. This island, rising on sheer cliffs of lava is an active volcano. It is one of the Lipari islands, according to myth the home of Aeolus, the God of the winds. Stromboli is only eight square miles and it rises 3000 feet out of the sea. I was surprised to learn that people actually live there, in spite of an ominous history and location. Stromboli lies in a line between the volcanos of Vesuvius at Naples on the mainland of Italy, and Etna on Sicily, two volcanoes which have erupted and killed often in the past. We were told that there are places where the sea actually boils from underwater volcanic action. The Lipari islands have been a place of exile for political prisoners since the time of the Romans. Yet, there are many tourists who come for the beautiful and dramatic scenery. And the seafood is supposed to be wonderful.

Blossom was a little sick from choppy waters in the morning but got up in the afternoon. Possibly because she didn't want to miss anything. We all knew it would not be long before many of us would be leaving this ship of fun and so each of us began to entertain in his rooms. Gladys and Russ had each entertained and today at three we all went to Larry's room for his party. We were impressed with what he was able to serve. There were seventeen of us and we enjoyed a large bowl of champagne punch, American cookies, and sandwiches, plus cigarettes. Yes, I smoked in those days and considered it the necessary and sophisticated thing to do. I was twenty after all.

Italy

We arrived in Naples at 5 o'clock and docked at a large pier. The Marslands got off here and invited all of us to come to their hotel. We said farewell to them and they told us to call them when we returned. They lived in New York City and were a lovely couple. We had good times with them and we began to feel a little sad at the ending of this voyage. We went back to the ship early as Blossom still felt a little low.

The purser, Emilio, found me and asked if we could have a visit. He was a man in his thirties, of average build, perhaps a bit overweight, with a moustache and a tight, white uniform. He spoke English well, with a "continental" accent. He had been most courteous to us on the trip, finding us a nicer stateroom than the one we were originally assigned, and of course had invited me to dine with him the second night out when Blossom was seasick. Since then, we had smiled at each other and exchanged pleasantries when passing on deck or in the corridors - it was another of the many polite and casual friendships I had made on board the ship.

Now we sat in the sunny lounge and visited. Somewhere in the conversation I said I liked the smell of his aftershave. He said it was cologne. It was the first time I realized that some men also wore cologne. It seemed fitting and very European to me. Emilio said that he had a little bottle of it which he would be glad to give me.

"Come," he said. "I want you to see my quarters anyway."

We went to a lower deck and into a sort of business lobby, a place I had been in once or twice. I noticed that the lobby was empty and it seemed very quiet. Off this lobby was a doorway with a curtain for a door. It was through this curtain he ushered me. His little living room was nice but small and he pointed to the next room. Have a seat he said as he rummaged through some bottles and I sat down on his bed.

He turned around and sat beside me and gave me a little bottle of cologne. All at once he pushed me over onto the bed and got on top of me. He was strong and heavy, so I could scarcely move. Alarm bells began to ring in my head. This is the way girls are raped and it's happening to me! When he lifted himself up a little to unzip his fly, I did what I had heard would hurt men. I raised my knee hard into his private parts and he groaned and fell back.

I was on my feet in an instant, pointing my finger at him and saying, "Not me!" in as firm a voice as I could muster. I was still aware of how quiet it was and didn't want to be loud and call attention to myself. It was a discrete little scuffle and it was over. I was on my feet and he was still on the bed, holding himself.

"I see we can't be friends," he said weakly, his accent sounding a good deal less charming to me now.

I didn't answer him. I just left and as I walked across the lobby, I tried to act nonchalant. I needn't have bothered — no one was there.

I hurried to our room and told Blossom what had happened. We both drew sighs of relief that I was all right. I looked down and discovered that I still clutched the bottle of cologne in my hand. My heart was still pounding, as I realized what a narrow escape I had made. I knew I would not meet his eyes again. I had learned an important lesson and with it came a feeling of sadness. The safe world I had known, where people were always as kind and friendly as they seemed to be had somehow slipped away. I was twenty years old and a woman. I would need to be stronger now, not so innocent and trusting as I had been. I had come a long way from Joplin, and in some ways, I would never go back again.

Blossom was my dear companion and confidant through this trip. We came to share and depend on each other in all matters of the heart. Like mountain climbers, we were tied together by a cord that gave us the strength and confidence to venture into treacherous terrain. Although we were naive, we could reinforce one another to dare the abyss of men and romance without losing our balance. So, on this trip we could accept almost any invitation with aplomb. We could count on each other. I was her safety net and she was mine. My misjudgment with the purser drew me closer to her and strengthened our bond. We played games, read to each other, shared secrets, even the mysterious shocking one of how babies are made.

We were never lonely. We had differences but agreed on our behavior. We knew we would not go too far with any boy. I can't say why this was so, for our Victorian mother never spoke of such things. It was just the moral code of that day. It was our close relationship and mutual support that enabled us to spend so much time with men on this trip without getting into deep sexual waters. Most young men of our generation respected that moral code of the time.

I had been tested at seventeen by Gary Manning. He was so handsome in high school, and I longed for him to ask me out. One spring day, after he had noticed and danced with me several times at a school banquet, he called and made a date. We went to a movie and then rode out to the countryside. High on a hill he parked the car and we got out and walked together. The beauty of the night with his arm around me as we sat on the grass gave me the kind of happiness that makes a young girl cry. And then it changed, he went beyond the kiss and touched me in a way that sent an alarm through me.

"No, Gary, not that." I meant it, and he knew it and pulled away. By his manner then and all the way home I knew that he had asked me out for that reason alone, not because he cared for me or even liked me.

Another event in my emotional education was Roger Pierce. He was tall, good looking and "sophisticated," or seemed so to me. I was nineteen and he twenty-five when we met; I felt ready to fall in love with just such a man. We dated and necked on the porch swing, and when he told me that he loved me and spoke of a life together, I believed him because I wanted to so much. Then, after we had been keeping steady company for a few weeks, Blossom came to me and told me that Roger had made a pass at her. I was shocked and deeply hurt that someone I had put my faith and trust in, someone who had asked for my love and offered his own, should be so false. It was an experience that would stay with me and keep me on my guard. That event with Roger was probably what sharpened my instincts and let me respond to the purser as quickly as I had. Blossom and I talked into the night. We agreed that I had been given an important lesson and had only had to pay a relatively small price — a bit of embarrassment. Our family had always drawn strength from a positive point of view, and by not dwelling on the negative at that moment we decided to simply put the whole ugly experience out of our minds. And I did. After leaving that ship, I don't think I gave that episode a thought for many years.

Naples

We were up at 6:30 the next morning for we had a day in Napoli. This time we went sightseeing with the Marslands and another couple. We rented a car and driver and visited Pompei, Sorrento and Amalfi. Lunch at a little hotel in Amalfi came with a grand view. It was perfect weather and as we ate, we had music from a group of native boys. One of the musicians was a jug blower who must have come from one of the many ceramics-making families in nearby Salerno, because the jug he blew was decorated with his picture in the glaze. The Amalfi drive, which winds along the very edge of the sea, is gorgeous. It runs for about 25 miles along the southern edge of a peninsula that runs from Salerno in the east to the famous Isle of Capri just off the tip in the west.

Every few miles along that coast there was an ancient stone tower built to alert people of the approach of Arab raiders. These raiders were Saracens, the infamous Barbary Pirates coming from that long African coast we had just visited 250 miles to the southwest. The Barbary Coast, now known as Algeria and Libya, has long been a source of trouble for Europe and even for America. You may remember our own naval history and the bloody battles our Marines fought on "The Shores of Tripoli." These Roman watch towers were built as the first line of defense for the rich cities of Pompeii and Herculaneum and other populations along the coast. The towers were visible to each other as well as to others on clifftops and mountains inland, so that warning fires could be lighted at the first sign of approaching sails.

These days though, those towers are only quaint landmarks to please the curious eyes of thousands of tourists who like us, come to enjoy the remarkable beauty of the warm Mediterranean. Surely the Amalfi Drive was a magnificent introduction to our year in Italy. We had our lunch in a lovely restaurant at the top of the cliff in the town of Agerola, with a matchless view over the Bay of Salerno. The water there is so blue it seems to strike at nerves beneath the tongue — as much a tang as a hue.

We were to sail from Naples at 5 pm, and we all gathered at the rail to watch this lovely land recede behind our wake. Everyone was interested in what the others had seen and bought. Then someone noticed that Miss Smith was not on board. Miss Smith was a slight woman of thirty-five or so, plain, shy and retiring. She kept to herself most of the time. Time for departure was getting close — they had pulled up all the gangplanks but one and now the last one was slowly being drawn in. At that moment we saw Miss Smith drive up in a cab. The pier had two levels, one at water level the other higher to which the gangplanks were attached. She was on this upper pier running out to the end in hopes of catching the last gangplank. By this time everyone on the ship knew what was going on and began to call instructions or encouragement to her. Slowly the ship moved away from the dock and we all knew they never go back once they have cast off. Such excitement. A cockney man about three or four people down the rail from us started to holler at her. He had a booming foghorn of a voice that rose above everyone else's.

"Tike the trine to Genoa! Tike the trine to Genoa!!"

While he was bellowing, someone led her down some steps to the lower level of the pier where there was a small boat waiting. They put her in that boat and started after us. By now we were going a pretty good clip and as we watched she came along side and our ship dropped a long rope ladder. That poor soul, with packages no less, grabbed the ladder and climbed that swaying rope to the first deck. Everyone cheered as crewmen pulled her aboard at last. We could all look up now and enjoy the wider scene as we pulled out of the harbor.

Of all the lovely sights we had seen on our voyage, by far one of the most beautiful was the bay of Naples that evening from the deck of the Vulcania. The setting sun gave a golden glow to what has been described as one of the most perfect harbors in all the world. In the background Vesuvius rises above the city in stately splendor, with golden hills arranged in a crescent around the bay like a royal retinue. The hills have their own attendants — Italian cypress trees, shaped like tall, dark flames, clustered on the slopes in groups as if placed there by the hand of a Renaissance master. The city itself gleamed white and golden in the foreground, and all this splendor set off against the blue, blue water of the sea.

We stood at the rail until the view diminished from our sight then hurried to our cabin to have a little party for our friends, before our last dinner on the Vulcania. That evening, in a fit of excess, Blossom and I ordered everything on the menu. It was all paid for, and good fun for our table-mates—though I did feel a bit guilty about the poor waiters whom we kept on the trot, bringing dish after dish for us to sample. We had found so many first experiences in these two weeks and we were reluctant to leave any part of this wonderful and exotic life afloat untasted.

Harriet

Harriet's Family

"February 6th. Today we will land in Genoa and for us it will be the end of this wonderful voyage on the Vulcania. The only port of call that we will miss will be Cannes as she continues her cruise. How grateful I am that our parents chose this ship." My diary records the end of that journey by sea but not the end of my gratitude to my parents for the generous foresight of their gift. I still savor it sixty years later.

Our sister Harriet and her husband Franco Emmer were at the pier in Genoa to meet us. Her life here in Italy is a story unto itself.

Harriet is the eldest of us, born in 1908. She will turn thirty while we are visiting. She has the best brains in the family except perhaps our mother who, as we always said proudly, "was born in Superior with a superior mind and finished four years of high school and four years of college in four years." Harriet did not move to Joplin with the rest of us in 1925 but stayed in Wisconsin to finish her last two years of high school while living with our grandmother and grandfather Short in Superior. Harriet has many talents but chief among them is a gift for languages. She knew German well enough to work as a translator, learned French in high school, and minored in Italian at the University of Missouri, where she took a degree in Journalism. She graduated in 1931 and her Italian teacher, whom she liked very much, suggested that she travel to Italy. But how?

"Well," he suggested, "why not get a job there?"

So, she applied to the Berlitz School of Languages in Venice where she was quickly accepted as a teacher. On the ship going to Venice she met Franco Emmer, an energetic Italian who was bright and handsome, and a year younger than she. Franco worked for the Walter Kidde Company and was returning from a business trip to the United States. They recognized something special in each other at once and two years later they were married.

Franco's family belonged to a religious minority in Italy—the Waldensians, a protestant sect that had been persecuted in prior centuries. For the first two years of Harriet's life in Italy, she was working in Venice at the Berlitz school and Franco was working in Milan. They got together on weekends and holidays. At last, after two years, just as her visa was about to run out and she would be forced to return to America, they were married. Harriet renewed her passport and maintained dual citizenship.

Now, in 1938, they had two little boys; Dickie, three years old, and Frankie, just born the year before. Our mother had come over in 1935 to be with Harriet while she gave birth to Dickie. Mother had been quite favorably impressed with the Italians — (she reported that they were reading Chaucer!)—and it was her visit that prompted our trip. After some correspondence and investigation of the budgets, Harriet and Franco invited us to spend a year with them. It had been seven years since we had seen our sister. I was only fourteen years old when she came to Italy.

Together Again

To say we were excited at the prospect of our reunion in Genoa is a great understatement. We arose early and finished packing our stateroom. We said goodbye to all our friends of two weeks with whom we had such good times. Then, ready at last, we went up on deck to watch the docking. As soon as we were close enough to identify people on the pier, we spotted Harriet and recognized Franco from his pictures. We all took pictures of each other across the narrowing strip of water between us. Finally, the ship was secure and the gangplank down. You can be sure we were the first ones off. Such warm greetings, hugs, tears and laughter.

Harriet took a good look at us and said, "Oh Blah! what good legs you have, and Becky you look like our brother, Dick!"

"No, you do," I replied.

Actually, we neither one of us really did, but after so many years we could see every spark of family resemblance.

Franco was handsome, gracious and in charge. He called a porter and then led the way to customs. The porter started to spiel off Italian as he neared us and I caught my breath, mind whirling—what did he say? Forgetting completely that Harriet could understand Italian perfectly, I was relieved and awed when she replied with a torrent of instructions. This was a new and different sister than the one I knew. How difficult it is to jump seven years in less than seven minutes.

Franco returned and said he could go through customs with us. Much relieved but still thinking of the ratty trunk full of food I asked him if it would go through without costing anything. "Oh, don't worry, I will tell them you are on a special diet and must have this to eat," he said. His reassuring manner, and his nimble imagination when dealing with the impenetrable Italian bureaucracy was something we came to rely on during the next twelve months. And he was right, they didn't open a thing.

Since the ship had docked at 6 a.m., Harriet and Franco had come from their home in Milan the day before and spent the night at a hotel. We had all been too excited to eat anything and we now found ourselves starved. We took a taxi to the train station and there had a wonderful meal at the station café. Franco, knowing we would have a lot of luggage, had decided to have some of our suitcases and the two trunks sent right to their apartment in Milan. Feeling free, unencumbered and well taken care of, we talked non-stop on the train and arrived in Milan about four in the afternoon.

Their apartment building was on Via Sidoli, near the center of the city. From the lobby we entered an elevator, a metal cage with fancy filigree spokes which gave the whole thing a feeling of lace. The apartment itself on the third floor had a spacious entrance hall, or foyer, with a marble floor, which was typically Italian even for a modest home. There were two bedrooms, good size kitchen with a back balcony, and a large living room. In this living room were two bed-sized couches where Blossom and I would sleep.

At the far end of the living room were French doors that opened onto a lovely balcony which gave us a wonderful view of the street three floors below. As for a place to put our things and dress, we used a very large closet at the end of the foyer. It was big enough to hold a chest of drawers, shelves and hanger space, mirror, a couple of chairs and our wardrobe trunk. This trunk had been Harriet's when she went to college. It stood up and opened on end; one side held hangers and the other side had drawers. The bathroom was very large by our standards, with marble walls. Wood was very scarce in Italy, and beautiful marble in a wide range of colors was plentiful. All told, we were very comfortable.

The children were just adorable. Dickie was very blond with large blue, blue eyes like his mother, and Frankie had dark hair and large brown eyes. We scooped them into our arms and couldn't get enough of them. They were not in the least shy. We simply fell in love with them. Chubby Frankie did not walk yet, was all smiles and cuddled easily. In fact, the poor child would not walk for a long time. He was born with a condition similar to polio that prevented him from developing normally.

Somehow his malady made us love him even more. It was a sadness that Harriet carried in her heart but never displayed. For our part, we never spoke of it out of deference to our dear sister—but sometimes at night we could hear her crying in her room and it broke our hearts.

There was a live-in maid! At that time servants were very inexpensive in Italy and most middle-class families had at least one. Ours was named Linda, pronounced Leenda. There must have been a room for her back near the laundry room but I don't think I ever saw it. She was young, late teens I should judge, and terribly excited to see the two signorinas from Amerrrrrica. Harriet had taught her to cook and she did a very good job of it. We ate on a table put up in the living room. The little boys ate earlier at a dear little table in the foyer. Then they were bathed and put to bed. We did not eat our evening meal until around nine o'clock. This arrangement gave us plenty of time to spend with the babies, helping Frankie eat in his highchair next to Dickie at the table.

Franco came home before the children were in bed and played and talked with them. It was a very happy time in the house with Linda fixing dinner, leaving us free to enjoy each other. The very fact of having this full-time maid in the home made all the difference in our lifestyle there and the one we had back home.

In Joplin we had a much larger living space. Ours was an old-fashioned two-story house with three bedrooms owned by our parents, on a street filled with similar middle-class dwellings on North Byers Street in Joplin. There was a garage on the alley behind the house and a small back yard with the garden. Daddy had set up a small workshop in the garage with a lathe and other tools. He loved tinkering so.

But we girls did almost all the housework along with our mother. Dinner time was a busy time for us, so now we felt we were in the lap of luxury, even though we didn't have as much room.

Our first dinner in Milan gave us a taste of how wonderful the food would be in the coming months. First, we had pasta with a light sauce, then came veal browned and seasoned as I had never known before, served with fresh peas that had been steamed and just before serving had been put in the pan in which the veal had been cooked, giving the peas a delicious flavor of the meat drippings. Then the green salad with vinegar and olive oil, the vinegar put on first and tossed so that each leaf was coated and then the oil and tossed again. All this served with the best bread in the world, heavy crusted and made into rolls, baked fresh every morning in a local bakery. So tasty. The next course was fruit. Brought to the table unwashed, with a large bowl of water into which each person dipped their fruit, this time grapes, before eating them. The idea was that you should not wash fruit that will not be eaten right away. This of course, was the custom at a family table. Restaurants and parties handled fruit differently.

Linda served the meal and, after she cleared the table, she wheeled in a large tea cart loaded with bottles of various liqueurs. Such a surprise, a family serving all these fancy liqueurs! There was one called Grappa, a favorite of Franco's, and when you drank it, from small little glasses, it had a burning kick to it, feeling hot all the way down. We had only one glass this first night with a lovely heartfelt toast to our grand reunion.

After dinner the Winfield's came to visit. Good friends of Harriet and Franco's, they were an English couple, older, with gray hair and a soft spoken, gentle manner. I liked them immediately. After they left, Harriet told us that they had lost their only child and never really got over it. It made me feel so sorry for them that I could hardly think about it.

It was 12 o'clock before we got to bed. In the dark, Blossom and I talked.

"Don't you love Franco?"

"Aren't the little boys just adorable?"

"Isn't Harriet darling?"

"Can you believe we are really here?"

"It's all wonderful!"

So, on this first night at Harriet's, we had lots to talk about. We had opened the door onto the balcony to let in the cool evening air. Soon we heard the voices of young men singing from the sidewalk. Via Sidoli was a boulevard with large apartment buildings close to the sidewalk lining both sides. As the young men walked through this canyon, it amplified the music and sent it echoing over the city. They sang songs

I didn't recognize, perhaps from an opera, harmonizing sometimes in three parts. We finally concluded that perhaps they could be members of a chorus or choir walking home after rehearsal. Milan is such a musical city—(we would eventually see opera at the famous La Scala opera house). Whoever these young singers were, they were loved by two visitors from America eavesdropping from our balcony high above. The voices floated up to us, a clear, high tenor rising above the rest. We listened, enchanted, as they passed and their music faded away. What a perfect welcome to Italy!

Finally, we slept.

Sophia

The next day at noon our trunks arrived. Our gifts and goodies for Harriet's family were well received and made a miniature Christmas of a Monday afternoon.

They loved everything. We spent the day settling in and that evening more company came to visit. Harriet and Franco had so many friends who politely came to call and meet us during the first days of our visit. Often Harriet invited them to stay for dinner.

The second night in Milan we went to Sophia Gallo's for dinner and took her the package I had picked up from her husband's office in New York. Arriving at her apartment, we were admitted by the maid and asked to wait in the sitting room. It was a room crowded with 'objets d'art' and souvenirs from her career on stage. Oriental carpets and dark wood were the main decorative motif—there was a gothic air about the place. It seemed like a set for a murder mystery. At last Sophia swept into the room in an energetic cloud of chiffon, perfume, and cigarette smoke. She was about 60 years old, a fairly hefty woman with suspiciously blond hair, large hands and long scarlet fingernails. Harriet had told us that she was a retired opera singer and she seemed to be on the verge of an aria at any moment. She called everyone "dahling" and greeted us with flamboyant gestures.

We sat on plump couches as she opened the box from New York. The Dr. Denton PJs were pulled forth and greeted like a sable coat— clutched to her bosom while she told of her sufferings these damp winter nights. It took some effort to contain our smiles as we imagined her clad in these immense, footed, "jammies."

Through the dinner she repeatedly interrupted her talk on the hardships of a marriage divided by the Atlantic Ocean, to express her profound gratitude for the favor we had done her. It was a bit overboard, since all we had done was stow her box under one of the beds in our stateroom. Nevertheless, she told us that we were to consider her our newest and dearest champion and friend. She was determined that we should meet some interesting men.

Several times in the coming months, she arranged little teas for us and two or three young men. We went to the first expecting a fun time with some young men, but we soon discovered that Sofia was stiff competition. The only subject that interested her was herself, and when anyone steered the conversation toward other people or things, she pouted like a child. Blossom and I soon realized that we were merely the bait to attract young men to her drawing room. After a couple of these "teas," we politely made excuses and declined.

Shopping

Every day was a new experience. Each morning we played with the children and were amazed to find little Dickie, who spoke both English and Italian very well, never getting them mixed up. He always spoke to us in English and became our interpreter. Blossom and I loved to shop for Harriet in the little stores that were close by in every neighborhood. There was one for pasta, one for dairy foods, one for meat, one for vegetables, etc. We took Dickie to interpret for us. He was quite an amazing child and absolutely beautiful with his blond hair and blue eyes. One time in a department store we turned away from him for a moment to buy something and when we turned around found a group of people surrounding him and exclaiming how "bello, bello" he was.

In the lateria after we had ordered a liter of milk, we were amused when the man asked if we would like to take our milk with us or drink it there. We couldn't imagine anyone standing in that little dairy shop and drinking down an entire liter of milk.

The Italian methods of packaging were new to us, too. Paper was very scarce. There were no sacks or bags as we knew in the States, so the shopkeepers used newspapers. I particularly remember one little woman who ran a pasta shop in the village on lake Como where we spent the summer. She was small, bent and bird-like with a heavy black dress that swept the ground, rather like the ones worn in our country in the early 1900's. Dickie was not there to interpret for us at that time, so we had to deal with her ourselves, using pantomime and trying to understand her heavy dialect. We were there to buy rice, which she weighed out and poured into the middle of a single sheet of newspaper. Then, with an amazing dexterity she folded the newspaper in half over the rice and starting at the lower edges near the fold she turned the paper inward, sort of rolling it toward the rice, moving her hands up along the sides, forming as she went a tight, neat little packet in the shape of a crescent moon. She even managed to twist the ends into a little handle at the top to carry it. She performed this with great speed, talking all the time. Blossom had spotted a little bug in the rice and commented upon it. With a little bite in her voice she replied that the bug was there when she bought the rice so we would have to buy it, too.

The millinery shop in Milan was another one of our favorites. We loved hats in those days—they were considered an essential element in the wardrobe of a well-dressed person, and everyone, men and women, wore them. Blossom and I each carried several in our luggage, stacked neatly in a couple of hat boxes the size and shape of snare drums. I still love hats and am sorry to see that they have all but disappeared as a fashion item. To my mind nothing betrays the impoverished imagination and taste of these times more than the ever-present baseball cap.

But back to the millinery shop in Milan in 1938. It was surely one of the smallest shops in the city. No more than five feet wide and six or seven feet deep, there was barely enough room for the milliner herself to stand. The double doors opened out onto the sidewalk and the customer stood there to choose from the selection of felt hats which hung from hooks on the doors, the rear wall and in a small glass-topped counter. There may have been some hats made in factories there, but the ones we were interested in were made in the tiny shop by the milliner herself. When you found one you liked, the milliner would put it on her own head to model it for you. Blossom and I were unhappy with this arrangement and we had to do some delicate negotiating to try them on ourselves. At last the woman relented and we each bought a hat.

Each morning we would get our personal chores done, run errands, and always take time to play with the children. After a large noon meal to which Franco came home, Harriet had much to show us so we would set out to see the sights. First, of course, was 'Il Duomo' as they call the great cathedral in the center of Milan. It is set back in a large, open square so one can appreciate its mass and scale from a distance. The Duomo is like no other cathedral in the world. It is made of white marble and has five thousand statues on it. Hundreds of them are atop spires of various heights and when lighted at night, it is breath-taking against the dark sky. My first thought on seeing it was that it looked like an immense pastry, like a wedding cake, elaborately decorated with frosting and confectioner's sugar.

The Two Clubs

We Three—Blossom, Harriet, and Me

I expect it must happen in any community of expatriates, that those
who share a common heritage or country of origin or language
would tend to gather. In Milan, we were introduced to two such
gatherings which became the source of many activities and friendships.

First, there was the British-American Club, which was composed of
English-speaking couples of a certain rank and status who had been

assigned to Milan as representatives of their various companies. The British dominated this group. They made me feel that I had stepped up in class as they were older, and spoke in a veddy, veddy British way. Harriet and Franco were not members of this club because Franco was Italian, though Harriet had friends among the wives and through them we were invited to attend several functions.

'The Club' that Harriet belonged to was made up of British and American women who had married Italians and a few women whose American husbands represented their firms in Italy. It was known simply as 'The Club.' When we arrived at our first meeting, and we were almost the last to do so, we followed Harriet's example and went slowly around the room greeting each person and shaking hands. Of course, this first time Harriet was introducing us, but it was always the same procedure; we went around the room and shook hands with each person. They were all very pleasant to us, making us feel at home—which, when I think of it, was what they were gathering to do for each other, as well.

It was strictly social, meeting once a month. A few brought knitting or some other sort of handwork, but for the most part they just enjoyed visiting in English. There were women from all over who shared stories from home, adventures in Italy and always trouble with servants.

We enjoyed 'club' every month and became good friends with these friends of Harriet's. While the meeting shifted from one apartment to another, certain things were consistent. At four o'clock we went into the dining room and sat down to high tea. It was always a very nice table, loaded with marvelous sandwiches, tarts, cakes, pastries and fruit. What a repast! The party would last several hours. When we left and took the bus home, it was dark.

These women were of various ages and backgrounds. While they all shared a common language, certain regional prejudices did arise from time to time. One woman from New York remarked favorably on my clothes. I had on my gray wool dress with soft accordion pleats in the skirt.

"That is a charming ensemble you are wearing, dear," she said. "Where did you get it?"

"In Joplin," I replied.

"Surely not," she said, looking closer.

"Oh, yes," I went on. "Our little department store sends buyers to New York, too."

This brought an elevation of the eyebrows and a second's pause. Then she turned to another American and said: "That's just it Doro; sometimes you can get nice things in the west." Doro smiled and nodded, but neither of them seemed fully convinced.

We laughed at this later, and the phrase, "That's just it, Doro ..." became our private code for anything surprising to others that came from our American provincialism.

This Doro was Mrs. Doro Ausenda and she was to become a particular friend of ours. Though an American, she looked very Italian with dark hair pulled back into a tidy bun, heavy brows, a 'Roman' nose and very expressive mouth. When we met her, I would guess her age at forty. She wore black-rimmed glasses and her jewelry featured large diamonds. She was married to Signor Ausenda whom we seldom saw. He owned a thriving construction business in Milan. They had four children and lived in a lavish apartment which occupied the entire floor of an elegant older building near the Duomo. The children had exquisite manners. I remember meeting Doro with her eldest, a well-dressed eleven-year-old boy, on the bus one day. The youngster shook hands and bowed with all the aplomb of a seasoned diplomat.

Doro always had the most delicious food at tea. It was "High Tea" and perhaps even beyond the British standard for that institution. The table was filled with fruit, sandwiches, caviar, cheese, tarts and scones, whipped cream and clotted cream. There was no liquor, only tea to drink. We were waited on by a starched, gloved and uniformed team of servants who whirled silently around us as though on roller skates. Doro was an excellent cook and in later years she would write a series of cookbooks, published in Italian.

Thirty-five years later I was again in Italy and paid her a visit. She invited Harriet and me to lunch and apologized for the meager meal. "I have a fair shrimp bisque," she said — a dietary restriction, apparently. "But there is a very nice crepe Suzette for dessert." As I write this in

1999, I hear from Harriet that Doro is still alive at 100 and still cooking.

Some of the other members who made an impression on us were:

Nelda Cappelli from San Francisco who was fun and talkative, liked to tell us about Nob Hill in San Francisco. Her mother-in-law was a fantastic knitter. She could knit a piece just the shape of a coat pattern for instance and then sew all the pieces together just as you would if you had cut the pieces out of cloth.

Marguerite Giesalberti the wife of the head of Readers Digest in Italy. He had written a large book about Christopher Columbus. I think I have a copy of his book. It is long and full of detail, but a bit dry. She was British, with auburn hair, a thin face and impeccable manners.

Rose Barsotti, young, in her twenties, very pretty, southern, (from Alabama) and married to a young Italian Army Officer. She was dark haired, sweet, slow talking, with a beautiful mouth and lovely even teeth. She was quiet and maybe we were too, for these older women, 10 to 20 years our senior, were all so outgoing, bright, and interesting and yet they were extremely kind and loving to us. This club gave Blossom and me a wonderful lesson in poise and social grace. They liked Harriet so much and I'm sure it was partly for her sake that they took us to their hearts;

Mrs. Galassi the wife of the head of AT&T Telephone Co. in Italy. She was German and made the best apple strudel I ever ate in my life. Mildred Spelvin was from New York, a pretty blonde, quite young and she was the one who thought it quite amazing that we could find such good-looking clothes in Missouri.

Italian Men

Soon after we got to Italy and the news of our arrival spread to those who knew the Emmers, a couple of young single men asked Franco if they could take us out. At that time young Italian ladies were not allowed to go out on a date without a chaperone. So, the allure was not us in particular, for they had not even met us yet, but the chance of being with young girls without a chaperone. Since there were two of us, and we were used to dating, when Franco asked us, we said yes.

When they came and Franco introduced us, we found they spoke no English. However, they were quite good looking and we reasoned the language barrier would push us to start learning Italian. So, we started out on this new adventure with all of us smiling at each other. In the elevator one of them said, "Voi Balla o Cinima?" Blossom and I looked at each other, "dancing or the movies" we guessed. Language plays no part in dancing, so we chose that.

They took us to a large ballroom, very nice with a good band. We had a great time and found that our dates were good dancers. Eventually I had to go to the bathroom. I had foreseen this dilemma and asked Harriet for the word. She taught me what to say. I turned to the one who seemed to be my date and said, "Dove il Gabineto?"

"Si, Si," he responded and led me across the room and pointed to a door. I went through the door and was totally surprised to be met by a man in a white uniform. I didn't have time to speak before he bowed, beckoned me to a stall, opened the door, pulled down the toilet paper to get it started and ushered me in. When I washed my hands, he handed me a towel and I felt so dumb and embarrassed because I had left my purse with Blossom and could not give him the tip which I was sure he expected. I just smiled, said "thank you" in English and got the heck out of there.

When I got back to our table, I found that the boys had suggested we go ice skating. We liked that idea and were having a good time trying to talk with gestures and acting out words. The ice rink was beautiful with tables just off the ice where we settled ourselves after putting on our skates. Blossom and I had done very little ice skating and were perforce the helpless females needing to be held up. They were both excellent skaters and seemed to like holding us in their arms while we smoothly sailed around. We loved it. We laughed to let them know we were having a good time.

Back at the table we started to discuss names. We carefully pronounced each other's names and one of the boys asked me what "Becky" meant. As best I could I explained that it was not my real name but a nickname, that my real name was Rebecca. They were silent for a moment, looked at each other and after exchanging a few words asked to be excused and went off across the ice. Left to ourselves for the first time, we began to discuss the whole evening and the fellas. We were having such a good time talking the whole thing over that we were not aware of how long it had been since the boys left the table. Finally, it became apparent to us that they had been gone too long and we began to worry.

Why were they gone so long? Would they come back? What had we said? At last, it began to dawn on us. This was 1938 and the purge of the Jewish people had begun in Germany and now also in Italy. It was my name. They thought we were Jewish. After nearly half an hour, we saw them crossing the rink toward us. When they got to our table, we felt the need to explain enough to make sure they took us home. Again, in halting Italian and gestures I told them in America Jewish names were given to children who were not Jewish and I was not. They acted like that was not a problem, but the evening was not the same. In a short time, they took us home and we never saw them again.

This episode brought home to me the terrible dilemma of the Jews at that moment in history. We, of course, had many Jewish friends in Joplin and I felt badly that I had to deny being Jewish. It was as though I had betrayed my good friends and neighbors.

Harriet and Franco

ife with Harriet and Franco was delightful and exciting—they were so outgoing with a very active social life. They were a good-looking couple—Harriet was small, about five foot, three inches tall, with brown hair and alert, intelligent blue eyes. Franco was about five-ten, well-muscled, and dark with his black hair slicked back from his handsome face. Their bright minds made them especially attractive to people and it was little wonder that they had made so many friends of all nationalities. Harriet's Italian was perfect — she was able to pass as a native during the war, and she was also fluent in French and German.

Franco spoke English beautifully, with only a slight accent. He was the son of an Austrian-Italian father and English mother. He was educated at the Italian Naval Academy and served in the navy as the interpreter for the fleet commander in Shanghai. When he got out of the navy, he got a job with the Walter Kidde franchise in Italy which was owned by Admiral Compario. This man was an honorary admiral, given the rank by a grateful Navy for his contribution as an industrialist.

Compario was a wealthy man but extremely tight-fisted. His wedding gift to Franco, his right-hand man, was a box of cookies! Still, he seemed to love Franco and made him the manager of the business. Among many other endeavors the Walter Kidde Company still makes all kinds of firefighting equipment and installs sprinkler systems in buildings and ships. In 1930, Franco was sent to New York to learn more about the business, and it was on the ship going back to Italy that he met Harriet.

Blossom and I saw Franco as sort of a "wheeler dealer." He always knew what he wanted and how to set about getting it. He had tipping down to a fine art. When he traveled on an ocean liner, and the state room had two beds, he tipped the purser to remove one of them so he would have more room. At the theater he bought the less expensive seats and tipped the usher to seat his party in the best seats. When he was sent a card telling him to register for military service at the time of the war between Italy and Ethiopia, he simply wrote "deceased" on the card and sent it back, trusting the Italian bureaucracy to accept this as a fact. Which of course, it did.

Franco wanted us to take part in all aspects of Italian living. Learning Italian was a top priority, but it was difficult for we were with English-speaking people a great deal of the time. So, Franco would send us on errands with specific things to do. For instance, he sent us to the "Duomo Square," on foot. We had to find our way, find a certain hunch-backed man selling lottery tickets, and buy two. It was considered good luck to buy from a hunchback.

One time when two Italian boys asked us to go tea-dancing on the roof garden of a large department store across the street from the Duomo, I wore hat and gloves as was the custom. It was a lovely place and as dusk was falling the floodlights were turned on the Duomo. This was the big attraction of this particular roof-top restaurant. We were having a great time, but with every dance the feather on my hat got in my partner's face. So, I took it off. Well to my horror, a waiter came over and said I had to put it back on. When I got home and told Franco, he was livid. He said, "Becky, the next time something like that happens to you, point your finger at that waiter and say 'YOU! are here so serve me and not to tell me how to dress!'"

Franco was proud of us and the way we looked, with our American clothes and silk stockings. We must have looked different somehow, for strangers on the street would call us American as we passed.

Franco told us one time, "You might as well do whatever you want to no matter how crazy, for no one will think much about it, they will just say 'Muh, Americanata!'" We asked, "What's 'Americanata?'" and he said, "If someone gets out in the middle of the intersection, wearing a red tie and dancing the jitterbug, people will say, 'Americanata! What can you expect?'"

There is no doubt that I am an extrovert. I always have been one and I cannot apologize for it nor wish myself to be any different. But there must be some national trait that makes Americans all seem somewhat exhibitionistic to the Europeans. We Americans carry our culture with us and, perhaps because of the freedom that we take for granted and the relative prosperity that we have always known we are never quite able to set it aside. This has led to a complex relationship with the rest of the world, especially the Italians. I learned on this first encounter with them on their territory, that we Americans are viewed with a wide variety of attitudes from adoration to condescension to hostility. I think it has to do with our free-wheeling style. After all, we are from a young country—less than two hundred years old, walking on streets well over two thousand years old. Perhaps we unconsciously display the shiny, new confidence of third graders who don't quite appreciate the superiority of their elders.

Another time Harriet warned us against feeling that all Italians wanted to live in America. "They are perfectly content here and have good, productive lives. It is only those who are discontent who flock to Ellis Island." Looking back now from my much older perspective, I see what an important lesson Franco and his countrymen were trying to teach me. I was so young and happy then, barely out of my adolescence, and I had not learned yet to be aware of my overweening pride and how I come across at times when I like how I look, or charm someone successfully, or see my country's flag. I may still commit these errors, but when I am able to live a little more humbly, I thank the Italians and hope they can forgive an extrovert for being an "Americanata."

'Contract Bridge' was all the rage during the Thirties. Blossom and I had learned at home from Mother and Father who were fond of card games of all sorts. Franco and Harriet were good bridge players. The four of us made a foursome and when there was no social engagement, which was not often, we filled the evenings playing cards.

Franco and Harriet's friends came often and it seemed to us that they were all interesting people. Among the first guests to come for dinner were Megan and Tino Comini. Harriet told us before they came that their little girl, Alexandra, had a great deal of trouble with her eyes and was being treated for crossed eyes. They had lived in Spain, where she was born, and for some reason the bright light of the sun on the white stucco buildings had affected her eyes.

When the Cominis arrived, I liked them right away. She was small, dark, vivacious and talky. He was quiet to a complementary degree, as is so often the case, with sparkling eyes and a warm smile. The evening was fun for the conversation ranged over many subjects. First, we talked about Spain, or rather they talked and we asked questions. They had lived in Spain for ten years and finally had to leave because of the civil war going on there.

It was a bitter war, as civil wars are. The future dictator was trying to bring fascism to Spain and in 1938 he finally succeeded. The regime was an ally of Hitler and the German fascists were against democracy and the freedom people had enjoyed under their king. As the liberal democrats grew weaker, Tino and Megan Comini could see the inevitable end and felt they should emigrate before it was too late. He was a photographer who made oil paintings from his photos, dressing the subjects in fancy dress to look like their ancestors. He was very successful.

Megan Comini was interested in the supernatural and had taken part in some experiments to prove or disprove seances. She told of one time when a group of psychics rented a hotel room, gathered there, locked the doors and windows, and sifted flour all over the floor. Megan said the flour covered every inch of the floor so that no one could come in without being detected. Then they held a seance. They turned out the lights, heard voices and rapping and when they turned the lights on, the flour was undisturbed. She made a believer out of me though Harriet and Franco seemed skeptical.

About five days out of the week, we went out or had company. Most days we had two and sometimes even three social events. In the mornings we always spent time with the little boys. That's when we sewed or knitted. I made a dress for Harriet on her sewing machine. Blossom did a lot of knitting - I knitted too, though not as well as Blossom - I hadn't her patience. We also learned how to do a special kind of embroidery called 'shadow stitch.' In shadow stitching the bulk of the stitch is on the back of the cloth, the color of the thread showing though the fine linen. It is almost a lost art. We used it to make handkerchief-holders. A "handkerchief holder" is a cloth envelope, lined and slightly padded, about eight inches square, tied with a ribbon. Ladies kept their hankies in them and I still do. They're a bit old-fashioned, I know. I get only puzzled looks from my granddaughters.

Busy Lives

There often was luncheon, tea at five o'clock, and an evening event, sometimes two. Let me quote from my diary to show how the days went.

Feb. 26th Sat. Linda, the maid, went to a wedding and was gone all day so we had lots to do. I sewed on a dress for Harriet and played with the children. Took a nice long bath and fixed Harriet's hair. In the evening we went to a party at the Galassi's. We had lots of fun, danced, played charades and other games. We showed them how to dance the Big Apple. They asked us to sing and they seemed to like it. The food we had was grand.

Sun. Feb. 27. Slept till almost noon. Had lunch and played cards. We went downtown about 4 o'clock. It was a holiday, the Ice Carnival, and there were a lot of people there. At five o'clock we went to Sophia Gallo's for a waffle tea. The Palucca's were there and two young men. They were both good looking and very nice. One was tall and spoke a little English. His name was Gofredo. After the tea which lasted until eight on account of making the waffles, Sophia, Gofredo and I went to a concert. Then we picked up Blossom, Harriet, Franco and another man named Katz, and went dancing. We went to the O'Milano—very nice. A Mr. Borsilino came over and spoke to Katz and wanted to meet us. He is a multi-millionaire and owns one of the largest hat companies in the world. He asked us to a party he was giving next time he was in town. Two others came over to meet us and dance. We had lots of fun. Gofredo is certainly handsome.

Jeff

In March the weather began to warm, and on a gorgeous day, Monday, March 7th, Blossom, Harriet and I took the boys for a walk. We did this as often as possible and on this day Frankie did very well. The day passed quickly and after a light supper we dressed to go to the British-American Club party. Harriet and Franco did not belong, but the Winfields had asked us to be their guests. It was held at the Vecchio Milano, a beautiful, intimate restaurant with a small dance floor and a good band. It was on a lower level than the street and as you descended a wide staircase, you faced a large mirrored wall on the landing. It was extremely elegant, and Blossom and I were excited and a bit awed as we swept down the stairs into a roomful of music and gowns and tuxedos. There were more English people than Americans and they were all extremely nice to us. As we danced with them and visited at the tables, it felt as if we were living in a play by Noel Coward. Their accents and phrases such as "My Dear Gull," or "Raw-thur," were so exotic to a couple of girls from Missouri.

It was a wonderful evening. Dinner was served at 11 o'clock and we danced until 2:30. There were a couple of single men there who gave Blossom and me quite a rush. We were talking at the bar when I finally realized that their accents were different from the English around us.

"Are you Scotch?" I asked Jeff, the taller of the two.

"Ach, nay lassie," he replied with a twinkle. He held up his drink, a tawny liquid without ice. "This is scotch, dinna ye ken? A single malt scotch, as a matter of fact. I, on the other hand, am a Scot. A single Scot with a wee more malt in me than I woke up with this morning." He laughed in a way that made it impossible not to join in.

This was Jeff Jephson and his smaller friend, Mac McKinsey. Jeff was tall, a rather large man in his late twenties, with sandy hair a little bit on the red side, laughing eyes, a droll mouth that would purse a little when he was joking, and a casual way of holding his cigarette. He looked great in his evening clothes, tails tonight, and he had an easy manner with everyone. I quickly learned not to call him 'English' but that since Scotland was part of the British Isles, it was okay to refer to him as a 'Brit.' It was evident all these Brits knew each other well, a very intimate clique, which is natural when in a foreign land.

While I was dancing with Jeff he said to me, "I would like to take you to tea, if you would like."

"I would like it very much," I replied.

"Very well, it's a go. I'll give you a ring tomorrow afternoon."

It was hard to get to sleep that night. Of course, whenever we stayed out that late, we slept late the next day and had company only for tea in the late afternoon.

Jeff called and asked me to tea the next day. It was fun to be with him and I loved the place we went to tea. It was called Biffie's and was in Milan's famous Galleria. Centuries before our covered malls, the Italians created one out of an intersection of two narrow streets between four equally tall buildings, by simply filling the space between the roofs with glass. They re-paved the streets with beautiful marble floors and presto, there was an indoor street—a mall. The Galleria is in the center of town right across from the Duomo. Right in the middle, where the streets crossed was Biffie's, with tables 'outside'—that's where Jeff and I sat. For some reason being with this sophisticated man made me feel like an independent American woman. He was very easy to talk to and we got along famously. I had the feeling that we would see a lot of him.

He said, "You two girls made a big hit at the Club the other night. I for one am so glad you are here. I hope you will let me take both of you out to dinner Saturday."

I was thrilled, this trip is getting better all the time. We talked about swimming and how the warm weather made me think of the wonderful pool at the du Pont plant in Joplin. It was fed by a clear, cold natural spring in the wooded hills outside the city. Since daddy was the supervisor at the plant, one of the perks of his work was that we were able to use this lovely private swimming pool. I told Jeff about that and how I hoped to find a place to swim here. He reassured me that the nearby lakes were famous local swimming venues and he would see to it that we went there in the summer. After lunch he even bought me a bathing cap! (I love it when men buy me things).

However, when I got home, I found out we could not keep the dinner date with Jeff because we are going to ROME! Harriet had received $100 from daddy and by the time I got home she and Franco had decided that when money came for us the best way to spend it was to go sightseeing. Harriet had been in Italy seven years and had never stopped studying about this country. Student that she was, in some ways she knew more about Italy than Franco did. She was especially interested in the history and art of Italy and, by sharing her expertise with us, enriched our travels greatly.

This was Wednesday and we would leave on Saturday. Thursday and Friday we worked at preparations to go. But the social life went on. We entertained two women for tea on Thursday, while Blossom was knitting furiously to finish a knit dress she was making for Harriet. Gofredo, the handsome young man we met at Sophia's, called and asked Blossom and me out for the evening. He had a friend named Adian who proved to be delightful. We went dancing and had a glorious time laughing over the fact that we spoke such poor Italian and they spoke no English. It was a good Italian lesson for us.

Franco had business in Genoa Saturday, so he left in the morning by train. We planned to meet him in Genoa, then take the train along the coast to Rome the next day. So, Saturday we all worked fast to get away on the 5:30 train. There was much to do to make sure the little boys and Linda were well fixed and had everything they would need while their mother was away. Linda is so efficient and good with the children Harriet had no qualms about leaving them.

By now Blossom and I had a warm relationship with Linda. It was much more fun to try to speak Italian with Linda who spoke no English—our preparations became a game, with lots of acting out, gestures and laughter. We hugged and kissed the three of them goodbye and took a taxi to the station.

We arrived in Genoa in a high mood. Franco met us and had the evening planned. We checked our bags and walked along the harbor where we saw the big S.S. Rex docked. We talked about Columbus leaving this very harbor. Franco wanted us to see what he called the "lowbrow" streets where the laundry was hanging out, windows open and Mamas calling to their children, their voices echoing through the streets.

We ate dinner at one of Franco's favorite places, near the harbor, a sort of hole in the wall place where he said they served the best fish in town. There was an air about it that added to our festive feeling of "Here we go on a vacation in the midst of our glorious vacation." Blossom and I loved the atmosphere, the checkered tablecloths, toothpicks that were pieces of whittled wood. And to cap it off, when they wanted coffee, the waiter stepped to the door and hollered across the street to a bar who then brought it over. After dinner we walked back to the station and got on the midnight train to Rome.

Rome

We were separated on the crowded train. Blossom and I found ourselves in a compartment with three men who spoke no English, but our little Italian got us acquainted. Sleep was hard to come by sitting up on the upholstered benches; (how I missed those Pullman cars back home) but we managed a few hours.

Franco's business associate, Mr. Adinolfi, met us in Rome and took us to a small hotel. It was a pensione, which was a hotel that included breakfast and dinner with the cost of the room. The bathroom was down the hall and had a tub that seemed to be seven feet long. However, it was inexpensive and served us well. We washed, had breakfast and Mr. Adinolfi came for us. It was chilly but we were prepared with coats, and that morning he gave us a whirlwind tour of Rome. It was even better than I expected.

We met Mrs. Adinolfi and her sister and parted from the men who went to work. We five women drove into the country where we had lunch in a quaint little town. This was another first for Blossom and me to be with two Italian women for an extended time, who spoke no English and talked so fast. They were delightful women, both very fashionable, hats and gloves and dressy clothes, petite, outgoing and spoke with such excitement. Mrs. Adinolfi was telling Harriet about something with great gestures, clipping the words off so fast, I was sure a great tragedy had occurred, perhaps a fire.

Finally, I could stand it no longer and asked Harriet, "What is she telling you?"

She replied, "A mutual friend's daughter has accepted a good job."

It was something of a burden for Harriet to interpret, so Blossom and I talked together giving them freedom to visit. Alone with Italians we did fairly well because they spoke slowly to us, but without Harriet there we were lost.

Because we had so little sleep on the train, we went to bed very early that night and slept late. In the morning, feeling refreshed we were ready to take on Rome. What an exciting place, and the beauty of it was that then, March 1938, there were so few tourists. The sky was clear and streets busy with tiny Italian cars, buses, and lots of bicycles.

The first thing Harriet did was buy a map. She made a list and planned our strategy for the five days we would be there. The first item was St. Peters. We walked inside. The enormity of it was astounding and yet everything about it was so balanced that the size eluded us. For instance, our guide asked us to look at one of the huge columns where marble doves were placed about head high. The guide asked us what size we thought the doves were. We were at the time some fifteen feet or so away. I said I thought his hat, a gray fedora, would almost cover the whole dove. He walked up to the dove and placed his hat upon it; the hat barely covered the feet.

This marvelous structure had one surprise after another. We saw it all—we even climbed up in the dome which was actually two domes. The inner dome which can be seen from the floor of the great cathedral, painted and decorated with magnificent frescos; and the outer dome which is one of the great landmarks of the world and can be seen from every part of the city. It is possible to climb the steps into the space between these two great architectural wonders.

Harriet stayed below and the guide came with us. Climbing all those steps in that cramped space gave me an uneasy feeling—this building was so old, and I was afraid it could give way. The space allowed for the steps was narrow, our shoulders touched the sides. It was scary. The steps follow the contour of the domes so that as you near the top you must bend sideways. When we arrived at the top, we found ourselves standing between the inner dome and the outer. Looking up we saw that we were under a small opening which led, by a metal ladder, to the golden ball that graces the top of that magnificent dome. As the three of us stood, squeezed together he asked, "Do you want to go up into the ball?" There were little slits in the ball so we could peer out and see how high we were. We had come this far so we said, "Si."

Blossom and I climbed the ladder and were at last inside this golden ball that looks so small from the street below. We took turns peeping out of the narrow slits across the city that was the center of the western world for so many centuries. The view took what remained of our breath away. It was not too many years later Harriet told us that they closed both the dome and the ball to tourists. I am not even sure if people are allowed on the roof to walk behind the giant statues of the twelve apostles that stand along the facade.

Alfredo's

We met Franco and the Adinalfis for tea, sitting in the warm sunshine at a small outdoor café on a busy street. Bicycles made up half the traffic, and many of them were delivering merchandise. The most unusual were two men on bicycles holding an armchair between them, balancing it like a circus act. It was the most entertaining traffic I had ever seen.

After refreshing ourselves at the pensione, Franco took us to the most famous restaurant in Rome—Alfredo's. At that time there was only one in the world and this was it. Years later when I went back to Rome, there were four Alfredo's, and no one knew which was the original. He was famous for his pastasciutta, "fresh pasta." The walls were completely filled with autographed pictures of every movie star, opera star or famous person you could name. The world had come to Alfredo's to dine. Franco ordered for us and as we sipped our wine, we discussed how essential the dining experience is to our trip. We were learning so much and having such fun doing it!

When our food arrived, Alfredo himself came to serve us. On a cart brought to the table were hot plates and a large platter of golden noodles on top of which were two large hunks of melting butter and an enormous amount of finely grated parmesan cheese. After Alfredo greeted us warmly, he took from his pocket a large gold spoon and fork and began to ceremoniously and with great flourish move the butter and cheese into the pasta with long strokes. He did it with such dexterity, never losing any pasta over the edge of the platter and mixing it thoroughly. Franco told us the gold fork and spoon were a gift from Douglas Fairbanks and Mary Pickford, stars the world over in silent films. I have never eaten anything in my life as good as that pasta. Today it is known as "Fettucini Alfredo."

It sounds so simple, you would think it could be duplicated, but Franco said, "Alfredo's is special because he has a certain pasta, a certain burro and certain cheese. You can't buy them."

But this was only the first course. After the pasta we were served fried turkey breast and asparagus with those wonderful Italian hard rolls and finally the Italian answer to the French crepe, an egg omelet with jam. Delicious! It was such a happy time. We loved Rome and Franco was so pleased that we did.

In the days that followed we saw all the "must see" places of Rome. Harriet was a wonderful guide for she is a student by nature and never stops reading about Italy. As I have mentioned before we were able to go where later the public was not allowed. The coliseum let us wander around inside and even go to the lower level where the Christians were held. waiting to meet the lions.

Having several days there and planning carefully, we were able to spend time and truly absorb and enjoy what we saw. In the Sistine Chapel we were able to take all the time we wanted to note and talk about each panel of the great masterpiece of Michelangelo's ceiling frescos. The day we were there it was almost empty except for six or eight German people and us. We had the leisure and freedom to stand there for an hour, gazing up at this ceiling that took the artist seven years to paint.

Harriet was a fountain of knowledge telling us how over the centuries the cardinals gathered here, camping, as it were, in this room, to select and vote on a new pope. It sometimes took weeks, and the little stoves on which they cooked their food smoked up the air and added grime to the magnificent ceiling. The cardinals could not communicate with the outside world and after each vote they notified the world of the outcome by the color of smoke. Black smoke, coming from a chimney, meant no agreement yet; white smoke meant they had elected a new Pope.

We did a lot of walking which enabled us to get a feel of the city, both the ancient parts and the modern streets and shops. We went to a street market where I bought a linen luncheon set for $1.75.

Mussolini

As we crossed a street Harriet looked down to the next corner and saw a row of cars and some men marching past. "Oh," she said, "Today is March 12th, isn't it? Some German veterans are here today, and I bet Mussolini will come out on his balcony." Well, we took off for that next street in a hurry, turned the corner and one block further found ourselves in a square filling up with people. Facing the square loomed a large, fortress-like building with battlements and a tower.

There was a window in the center of the second floor with a railing and a small balcony. This was the place from which the dictator often waved to the masses. On this day we were among those masses; a "front-row seat" if you will. The crowd buzzed expectantly repeating the words "Il Duce" (Eel Doo-chay), Italian for "The Leader."

Next to us stood several excited young men who listened to us talk among ourselves. Finally, one turned to us, held his hand in the German salute and said "Heil Hitler."

Aghast, I replied quickly "Oh, no, we are not German, we are American."

He smiled and said, "Then, Heil Roosevelt."

About this time there was a slight movement of the doors opening onto the balcony and the crowd went wild, chanting together "Du-che! Du-che!" It was a deep-throated roar and it had a hypnotic effect on me. I wanted him to come out. I wanted to see him! To my own amazement found myself chiming in with the throng, shouting "Du-ce! Du-ce!" I learned in that moment how easy it is to get caught up in the delirium of a mob.

At last the doors opened and Mussolini came out onto the balcony. He was stocky with a full chest, straight posture, ruddy face and a broad smile with flashing teeth. He wore a tight-fitting uniform without a hat, his shaved head shining in the Roman sun making me wonder if it had been polished. The crowd erupted in a mighty roar at his appearance and his chest seemed to inflate with their energy. I should say 'our' energy because by this time I was yelling along with everyone else. I felt I was standing on the edge of the world stage, part of the power of this cocky little man on the balcony. Mussolini saluted the crowd with an outstretched hand.

I looked at him closely. I had never seen a man with this kind of personal energy. His manner was one of unrepentant conceit. It seemed the word "vainglorious" must have been coined just to describe him. And yet, there was a certain appeal to him. He was so happy, so pleased with himself that you almost wanted to laugh. He grinned and basked in the adoration for a few minutes, saluted again to another mighty roar and then, like someone declining a third helping of dessert, he left the balcony and was gone.

The Black Shirts and Becky

For the crowd in the square it was as if a curtain had come down on a great stage performance. Everyone was nodding and smiling and talking to one another. The soldiers seemed newly aware of their uniforms and were carrying their chests higher and stamping their boots with more authority on the marble pavement. Looking back on it now, it seems ominous and dangerous, that crowd of men eager for battle and glory. But at the time, to girls fresh out of Missouri, it all had the air of a rather elaborate high school pep rally.

"I want my picture with these soldiers," I said to Harriet giving her my camera.

"Okay, get in there!" I did so, but only just. When Harriet called out "Signori!" to get their attention for the camera and she snapped the picture. You can barely see some of my face and left leg behind the crowd. No one in that gang of Black Shirts seemed to notice me.

Rejoining my sisters, I suddenly realized something and I said to Blossom, "TODAY we should have worn our riding boots and jodhpurs!"

"Yes!" she said, laughing with me. Then turning to Harriet to explain the joke: "We got those boots and jodhpurs to party with our Joplin high school girlfriends - dressing up like the rich horsey set... And those are the very things worn by Mussolini's Black Shirts!"

It struck us as so funny, we had to sit down on a handy bench and laugh and laugh.

"Do you suppose they'd invite us to their party?"

"Would we want to go?"

As we laughed, Harriet tried to calm us down.

"Shh! Let's sober up now," she implored.

As the stern-faced men stamped off, giving us puzzled looks and dignified frowns we had to stifle ourselves lest they realize we were indeed laughing at them.

"Hmph! Silly Americanatas," we could see them thinking.

We regained our composure and walked away—but every now and then, throughout the day, one of us would mention "Boots and Jodhpurs!" and set off a new round of giggles.

What next?

"I know, "Harriet said. "Let's take the circamvalacione"

"What's that?"

"It's a tram that circles the city and we will get a good idea of the outer Rome."

It was a wonderful time to sit and see and talk. In fact, our speaking English caused all the passengers to talk about us. They were mostly ordinary folks and workers going home. Harriet told us they were saying that it was disgraceful for the rich Americans to come over here and take the poor peoples' seats on the tram. To the Italians we were always the rich Americans. Rich or poor, we were tired and the hour's ride around the city was a welcome relief.

Our day ended with ominous news. Refreshed from the tram ride through the wonderfully warm afternoon, we decided to mosey around the ancient ruins. As we walked toward a statue of one of the Caesars, we noticed a group of young men about our age gathered nearby. There were seven or eight of them and as we drew near Harriet heard them speaking German. They had cameras and were trying to get each other's' picture in front of this statue. Harriet spoke up in their language and offered to take their picture all together.

They did not seem to be in the holiday spirit of most of the tourists we had seen but were in serious discussion. However, one of them thanked Harriet and handed her his camera. As a sort of routine question, she asked them where they were from. They exploded into a torrent of German, all talking at once.

"We are from Austria, and we have just learned that Hitler has declared 'Anschluss' and marched his troops into our country today."

"What?" Harriet was horrified. She quickly explained to us that 'Anschluss' in German meant 're-unification' and that essentially Hitler had annexed Austria and made it part of Germany.

Harriet spoke German quite well, and they gathered round her and wanted to talk about it. They were frightened and angry and as Harriet translated for us the boys nodded and asked where we came from.

We said, "America."

They all sighed and said, "Lucky, lucky."

As we walked away Blossom and I asked worriedly, "Will there be war?"

"I hope not," said Harriet. "Who knows?"

"How would we get home?"

"Well," Harriet laughed, "you might have to go home on a U.S. battleship."

Blossom and I looked at each other for a moment, and then both together said, "That might not be so bad!"

Rome was filled with men in uniform, some wore a handsome blue-grey uniforms with lots of gold braid and others in dark navy blue. There were three officers at the next table at dinner that night in the Pensione. They could hear us and we them, so, to test if they understood English, we said something very shocking such as "I read Roosevelt died last night." Since there was no reaction, we knew we could speak freely. They, on the other hand, didn't know Harriet spoke perfect Italian.

Harriet translated for us—and they were talking about us. Their comments went something like this.

"Look at those Americans. You would know them anywhere."

"I wonder what they are doing here?"

"I don't know but they are lookers all three."

"Yes, I would like to have them in my room one at a time, from the oldest down to the youngest."

"I wish we could meet them."

It was hard for us to keep from giggling as Harriet told us what they were saying. We finished dinner and were in the lobby when they came in and all smiled. Blossom pulled out a cigarette from her purse and started to dig for a match. Up stepped one of these officers with a lighter and that broke the ice. They were struggling to communicate when Harriet spoke up and said, "We can speak Italian if you like." The look on their faces was just what we expected, but the twinkle in our eyes let them know we were not offended, so we all sat down and had a nice visit.

These men were about 30 years old and very polite with fair hair and fine features. Of course, the uniforms didn't hurt their looks any. Blossom and I at 22 and 20 thoroughly enjoyed the hour we spent in conversation with them.

Before we left Rome, Harriet wanted us to see the 'Wall.' This wall had five enormous maps of the whole Mediterranean area. They were made of stone or cement and the sequence showed history of the Roman empire. The first had only a white dot for Rome. In the second the white area had grown to include all of Italy; the land on the east side of the Adriatic, Sicily and the Italian Islands, and the Iberian Peninsula. The third map showed the great Roman Empire at the time of the Caesars. The white surrounded the whole Mediterranean Sea and beyond. The fourth showed a loss of white but still there was a great deal of land under the control of Rome. The final map was of 1938 where the white was of Italy, Sicily, the Islands, Libya, Tunisia, and Ethiopia. The idea was to give a graphic representation of Mussolini's ambition to restore the great Roman Empire again.

On our last day in Rome, Franco joined us again. He had gone back to Milan for most of our stay. While he and Harriet slept late that last morning, Blossom and I woke early and took a bus back to see St. Peter's again. We wanted to look one last time at our favorite pieces of art in this most unusual treasure. Mine were two. One was the marble carving "The Pieta" done by Michelangelo 400 years ago. It depicts Mary holding Jesus in her lap after He has been taken down from the cross. It is so moving, and I could not imagine the skill required to take away just the right amount of stone from a huge block of marble and leave this smooth, almost living statue.

The story goes that after it was finished and on display someone credited it to another artist. This so enraged Michelangelo that he went in the dead of night and carved "Michelangelo Buonorotti Made This" in the ribbon that angles across Mary's chest.

My other favorite work of art in St. Peter's is a large picture of Christ standing near a pool with one foot half immersed in the water. It is a huge picture and seen from a distance looks so very real with soft colors and the foot in the water is diffused just a bit. The shock came, when first I approached and saw that it was not painted but made of little pieces of colored stone cemented together with wonderful delicacy and craft. My attention was especially held by the rendering of Christ's foot in the water. The colored bits of stone and glass in this mosaic, though hundreds of years old, have not faded. They were placed so closely together with such subtle shading that they gave shape and volume to the flesh and a transparent liquid surface to the water. I was so glad we had gone back. For seeing wonders, once is not enough.

Florence

We arrived in Florence about noon on March 20th. Two months ago today we sailed from New York. Lunch was the first order of the day and Franco said we must go to the Buca de Dante, the 'Hole of Dante.' The food was excellent and afterwards we visited Dante's home. At times it seemed unreal that I was walking and seeing places that belonged to famous people of the past. Names that were only names before, heard in history class or taught in Literature 101. We crowded a lot into two days, Harriet again being the perfect guide.

The Renaissance began here in the 14th and 15th centuries, leaving us much to see in this jewel of a city. Of course, we could not see it all, but we hit the high spots. We went at such a pace that Franco finally called for a rest and sit time in the Piazza Della Signoria, which is a large square facing the Palazzo Vecchio, a fourteenth century castle. This housed the government of the city until 1532 and it's still the town hall. On the square were several cafes with outdoor tables where we had our tea. The day was warm and sunny and while we had our tea and rested our feet, Harriet and Franco told us fascinating stories of Florence.

In front of the Palazzo Vecchio just across the piazza from where we sat, stood the famous statue of David by Michelangelo. Harriet told us this immense statue was carved from a huge block of flawed marble. The flaw was due to another sculptor's misjudgment for a previous commission and the immense block of Carrara stone had lain in the quarry for over 26 years. All the great artists of the city were given a chance to make proposals on what to do with the stone. Some proposed simply cutting off the damaged portion and carving a smaller statue. Michelangelo showed how he could incorporate the flaw by setting the legs and knees at that point. He was awarded the commission and spent four years carving.

When it was finished and set in the square, all Florence immediately recognized it as a masterpiece. At the unveiling a top official in the city who wanted to show his importance made a remark that the nose was a little too long. Whereupon, Michelangelo climbed a ladder, chisel in hand, and taking some marble dust out of his pocket, pretended to carve. The dust fell, the city official crossed his arms, nodded, and said, "That's better." As Harriet finished telling us this story, Franco quipped, "There you see the relationship between art and politics."

I'm sure that it was only a sweet coincidence that our mother, daughter of a Presbyterian minister back in Superior, Wisconsin should have the same name, Florence, as this special city. And that was also Blossom's true name, as well. Since our trip here was originally our mother's idea, we three daughters toasted her with glasses of Italian wine and agreed henceforth to consider this city of Florence our fourth sister.

This beautiful city was like no other in the world, and we hoped to come back. We did go back again and again years later, bringing our families with us. The original David had to be removed from the square and housed in a beautiful, air-conditioned room away from the elements that were eroding the marble. In its place on the square now stands an excellent reproduction.

Milan Again

With Jeff

It was good to get back home and see the children again. Linda had spent a lot of time cleaning and had the house sparkling. It didn't take long to get back into our social life. Jeff called and asked Blossom and me out to dinner Wednesday. When he called for us, he had Mac McKinsey with him, whom we had met at the British American club. We had dinner at Giannini's, a marvelous restaurant. Afterwards we went to the Embassy club to dance. The four of us hit it off and had fun planning another outing. Since we were in Rome on Dickie's third birthday, March the 15th, we had a party for him on the 27th. He didn't seem to mind in the least. Seven children and their parents came for tea. Dickie and Frankie looked adorable in their new suits and Blossom and I had fun decorating the cake.

Throughout this trip I've kept notes in a little red notebook some-one gave me as a going away present. It had the words "Scribble Book" stamped in gold on the cover, and that's how I thought of it. At the end of March 1938, I have written: "Spring is here, and the days are perfect. We take the children out to a park as often as possible. We have tea on the balcony and enjoy life immensely. Each week we see something new and Harriet makes sure we don't miss what we should know."

One of the greatest blessings of this whole trip was the gift our sister Harriet gave us as our tour guide. She had a talent for knowing what the true masterpiece was, the story behind the art, the history of the places. She absolutely loved Italy and made it her study, her work, and her play for more than the seventy years she would live there. I once asked her, "Harriet, how can you know so much about this coun-try and its art and history?"

"I read," she replied. "I always have a book on my bedside table, and it's often about Italy."

In this as in so many ways, Harriet reflected our mother. Like Florence Short Fahrig, her eldest child had the same superior mind, the insatiable curiosity, the taste, and skill for music. Harriet also played the piano like Mother and, perhaps going a bit overboard, she even played the accordion as well.

She introduced us to many first experiences—Grand Opera being one. "Milano" is home to one of the greatest opera houses in the world: 'La Scala', which means "The Steps"—I suppose because the audience rises in great rows like a glittering staircase filled with beautifully dressed humanity.

Wagner was Harriet's favorite composer, and when his great series of four immense operas called 'The Ring of the Nibelung' came to La Scala she bought tickets for the 'The Valkyrie' for the four of us. Although it was sold out, she was able to get standing room on the fourth tier. Good thing we were young. The Valkyrie is heavy and long, and near the end I began to feel a bit woozy. Looking down from our high perch, standing behind the last row in that hot, close balcony, listening to the ride of the Valkyries, it suddenly seemed as though the white shirts of the men in the orchestra below were throbbing in time to the music. I must have wobbled into Harriet because she quickly asked Franco to take me out for air. It was exactly what I needed. I soon recovered and was back with my sisters.

I must admit that in this respect I could not keep up with my brilliant eldest sister. I found four hours of Wagner's magnificent music came close to my limit. To sit, or even to stand (God help us!) through the over twenty hours of the entire "Ring Cycle" seems like devouring an entire chocolate cake by oneself. Still, it was important to Harriet and she was our host and we loved her dearly, and love comes with its own set of punishments and rewards. In the end, I judged the rewards splendid and the punishment tolerable. The thrill of being in that magnificent opera house made up for any discomfort.

It so happened that a friend of Harriet and Franco's saw us there and was so impressed that we would stand all the way through the four hours of that opera that he gave us his two seats for 'Siegfried,' the following opera in the series. Harriet was delighted and said, "The seats are very wide and plush, so the three of us can sit very comfortably on two seats." Franco graciously declined to go.

So, we bought one standing room ticket to add to the two seats and went to see Siegfried. We went to our appropriate level, which was below the one we had stood on and found our seats. But alas, they had a post between them. What to do. Well, we came up with the idea of offering our one seat on the stage side of the post to the person sitting next to our seat behind the post. Luckily it was someone most agreeable, and Harriet was right; we three fit very nicely on the two seats. We loved it all.

April

On April 1st it was Harriet's turn to host The Club. Blossom and I made cookies, Harriet made a grand nut-cake, and the meeting was a big success.

Little Frankie was teething and felt bad, so we spent a lot of time with him. Blossom and I always had lots of hand work to do – knitting sweaters for ourselves and the children, embroidering blouses and hanky-holders. We never sat around doing nothing.

On Sunday, April 3rd we spent a glorious day with Jeff and Mac. We went to Switzerland taking an eight a.m. train, then a boat and finally walking several miles to Lugano. Actually, the last couple of miles we got a ride from some nice man. The day was beautiful and Switzerland, as we expected, was neat as a pin. Mac and Jeff were so nice and often came to the house in the evening to visit all of us or have a game of bridge.

The days were warm and beautiful and filled with activity, but even so, I got my first real siege of homesickness. It was partly because my birthday was coming up on the eleventh, and I got a letter from mother. I couldn't wait to open it and for a time I longed for home. I could see her sitting at the desk that daddy had made for her. My mind went back to that Christmas I was 13, when we helped him bring the desk up from the basement. My father always loved making things and he used his early training as an apprentice with the cabinet maker to create a beautiful desk. To keep it secret from her, he had made it while at the du Pont plant and hidden it in our basement. Then, early Christmas morning, while mother was still dressing, we brought it up the stairs.

Blossom and I took one end and Daddy the other as he cautioned us to "be careful turning the corner." We put it in the parlor near the Christmas tree, then stood back and admired it. "Oh, it is beautiful, she will love it." We helped him wipe the dust off and felt the smooth grain of the black walnut wood. It was a narrow, compact piece of furniture—a writing desk meant to fit into the parlor which already had a piano, sofa and two armchairs. In fact, it coupled nicely with the other piece of furniture she used most, the small baby grand Steinway.

The wood was from a tree on the plant grounds that had been cut a year or two earlier and dad had it sawed into planks and stored to dry. He knew he would build mother a desk from the moment they cut down the tree, and he carefully watched over every step in the process. It took months to make and when it was finished, he smoothed it with pumice stone and oil and then gave it several coats of wax, rubbing it well until it had a satin glow. We put a ribbon on it and closed the big pocket doors to the parlor to surprise her as she came downstairs. She was thrilled.

Now in Italy I read her carefully written letter and felt beyond the words how she longed for us too. She wrote there was an emptiness in the house, and it was too neat – no bobby pins lying around, and it was far too quiet. I finished the letter, handed it to Blossom to read and went to our closet for a good cry. Maybe it was necessary to weep away my sadness—by the time my day came I was over the inevitable sorrow that marks the end of childhood and willing to accept the responsibility of becoming an adult. In my heart, I declared myself equal to the task, and had a wonderful 21st birthday.

Mother, Daddy and Gram sent me cards and five dollars. Blossom gave me a blouse and a lovely note calling me the sweetest sister in the world. Linda gave me flowers, Harriet and Franco gave me a knitting basket filled with gardenias, and the babies gave me a little pink basket filled with blue forget-me-nots. There was a lovely cake with 21 candles – I am now a grownup!

Water Sports

One day when we were downtown, we stopped by Franco's office and met Admiral Compario. He owned the business and was Franco's boss. He was a nice-looking older man whom Franco described as rich as Croesus and tight as Midas. Whenever he and Franco were to meet someone across town on business, Franco, always pushed for time, would take a taxi, but the thrifty Admiral would ride his bicycle.

The day we met him, his son, Monfredo, was there. He was just a couple of years older than we and terribly good looking. We visited awhile and he asked if we could type. Yes, we could. So, we made a deal. He would teach us Italian and we would teach him to type. This worked very well for a while but fizzled out when our free times were never the same.

It was at this time of the year, early April, that Harriet and Franco started thinking of where to spend the summer months. The custom was to find a house somewhere near one of the Italian lakes, or near the mountains where it was cool, and move there for the summer to get away from the heat in Milan. The men came up from the city by train for the weekends—few people had cars.

A good friend of Franco's named Pancotti did have a small car. We had not met Pancotti even though he was one of Franco's best friends. Finally, Franco ran into him one day on the street and he related the conversation they had.

"Hey, Pancotti, where have you been?" said Franco. "I haven't seen you in weeks!"

"I've been busy," Pancotti replied. He was a small man with thinning hair and a florid moustache.

"What do you mean busy? I want you to come over and meet Harriet's sisters from America."

"No thanks."

"No thanks? What kind of answer is that from a friend?"

"I heard about these sisters-in-law. You're not going to marry me off so easy, friend or not."

"Marry you off? Where did you get such a crazy idea? "

"It wouldn't be the first time someone's tried that..."

"I can't believe this."

"I'm not so quick to put my head in the noose."

Franco just looked at him for a moment. "You figure you're quite a catch, I see."

"I'm a happy bachelor, that's all."

"And you have been for nearly forty years now," said Franco.

"May God send me forty more."

"All right." said Franco. "I will make my sisters-in-law promise not to try to marry you. Will that be good enough?"

"I have your word as a friend?"

"My solemn word."

"Well, okay then."

On Easter Sunday, early in the morning, Pancotti picked us up for a trip to Lake Garda. Blossom and I had enjoyed seeing the cars in Italy—so strange and different from what we were used to ...and so small. There was the "Topolino" which means "Little Mouse" in Italian, and which was a tiny two-seater with only three wheels. In fact, I think I have seen larger tricycles. Pancotti's Fiat was larger than a Topolino, but not much. It seemed like something out of the funny papers to me. We just managed to fit the five of us into it—men in front and we three sisters in the back. We drove north, to the lake country.

We had packed a picnic lunch which we all enjoyed—we even roasted some of the marshmallows that we had brought from America. It was a lovely clear day. We could see the mountains to the north and Lake Garda sparkling in the sun. We walked around the little villages looking, in vain, for just the right villa to rent. We enjoyed riding in a car again and sang all the way home. Singing was something we had always done while doing the dishes as girls. Blossom and I harmonized together which always made the chore more pleasant. Harriet and Franco liked to sing and Pancotti added a good tenor. The only trouble was we seldom knew the same songs, so we took turns entertaining each other.

Milan Adventures

Every week seemed to bring something special. One week we went swimming in one of the city's indoor pools. It was something we had done all our lives, and with Missouri summers so hot and humid, we had almost lived in the pool. The pool at home was actually on the du Pont grounds just outside of the plant itself. It was created in the woods where a natural spring ran clear and cold. It was available for all the plant people, though many of the workers preferred the nearby river. Since there were only about six men on the staff during the Depression, the pool was like a private jewel to us. A very rare thing to have in those years.

In Milan the Olympic size pool was indoors and very popular. We were sitting on the edge when a man came up to us.

"You swim very well," he said.

We thanked him and were glad he spoke fair English.

"Would you like to join our club?" he continued. "You could swim free as often as you wanted."

We looked at each other and asked, "How much does it cost?"

"Niente. (Nothing!) We just want our club to grow and we want you on our swimming team." Well, that sounded good, why not? So, we signed up. He said he would send our official membership cards to us. When our cards came Franco looked at them and gasped.

"Mama mia, you have joined the Dopolavoro! The Fascist Youth Organization!" We kept our cards for mementos but never went back to the swimming pool.

Another time, Harriet and Franco ran into an old friend of theirs named Barry who worked at the Milan rowing club. I am not sure of the name but the club was something like the athletic clubs in our American cities. This one however, was situated on one of the large canals of Milan and included rowing or sculling in the activities. Barry was delighted to meet us and asked us to come to the club and take a boat ride with him. We made a date and later Harriet told us that he had been the champion sculler of the world.

We did go to the club and he took us out and gave us a lesson. He was English and so nice, and in June invited all of us to a big reception the club was having for Field Marshall Badoglio, who was Mussolini's chief of staff. Harriet told us ahead of time that Badoglio had been a hero in the First World War and led the army during the Ethiopian campaign. We could not know then, of course, that this tall, distinguished man with the medal around his neck would succeed Mussolini as Prime Minister of Italy in 1943. It would be Badoglio who would surrender to the Allies and then declare war on Nazi Germany, thereby saving the Italian nation great death and destruction. My impression of him was steel grey hair, a precise, military bearing, a red sash that ran diagonally across his chest—he kissed my hand and clicked his heels together.

I felt very much the provincial girl from Joplin for a few moments with the champion sculler of the world and the ranking general of Italy in this ornate room paying me polite attention. But then the orchestra began to play and Franco was there to dance with the three of us. Before long, I was dancing with one handsome man after another and enjoying this glittering start to my twenty-first year.

Hans Block

"Girls, there's someone I want you to meet," Franco was home early that day.

"Great!" we chorused, glad of a little relief from our sewing.

"His name is Hans Block and he's a Jew trying to get to America."

"How can we help?"

"He's been studying English and wants to practice in conversation with you."

"Wonderful!" Franco had all our attention. "Conversation is our favorite thing to do!"

At 2:00 the next day, Hans came to the door. He was a small man with a thin beard, bright eyes, and an eager smile. He carried a rucksack and a large flat briefcase that we later realized was his portfolio.

"Come in!" We offered to shake hands, but he hesitated, first wagging his hand at us, then changing his mind and taking Blossom's hand with his fingertips, as though it were a porcelain teacup. Then he took mine in the same tentative way.

"Forgive me," he said. "I'm not used to shake a woman by the hand."

"That's okay," I said, "Won't you sit down?"

"We're just going to have tea," said Blossom. "Would you like some?"

He nodded, accepted tea and a seat on the couch, taking off his large black hat and revealing a little black sort of beanie underneath. The beanie stayed on.

"I have such gratitude to meet you," he told us when he had his tea. "I hope to travel to America. Please if you would teach me something America."

"Well. First of all, your English is very good," I said.

"Yes indeed," said Blossom.

"What will you do in America?"

"Make pictures, hopefully," he patted his large black case.

"What kind of pictures?" we wanted to know.

He unzipped the black case and began to spread his photos on the coffee table.

"Ah, you're a photographer!"

"Ja, photographer," he shrugged and dropped his head. "I was in business —advertising."

"These pictures are lovely," Blossom said. "So sharp and clear."

"Good camera. Leica." And he reached into the rucksack and brought out a small silver camera.

"I wanted to photo the Riviera in Cannes but winter was not the season, so I went to Egypt."

He brought out some large photos of camels in a caravan, Arabs on their prayer rugs, and soldiers in the foreign legion with their distinctive caps.

"My goodness," said Blossom. "You have had some adventures!"

"Yes, the Arabs were nice to me," Hans said. "I traveled with them for two months. They loaned me robes and sandals and accepted my pictures as payment."

"I love these shots of the legionnaires," I told him. "Especially this one." I held up a stunning photo of a legionnaire on a sand dune, his hat cloth blowing as he scanned the desert for possible enemies. "It could be a picture from the movie Beau Geste!"

"The only problem was the food," Hans said. "I had to go to the hospital because of the food." Hans was two months on this caravan and ate their spicy food which he said was mostly made from corn. After his trip with the Arabs, he had to spend a couple of days in the hospital for his digestive problems.

(You may be wondering how Hans could travel so freely in Fascist Italy, which became a close ally with Nazi Germany. Research tells that Mussolini's government was not antisemitic in 1938. Only in 1940 did the Italian government enter the war and begin deporting Italian Jews to the Nazi camps.)

When we asked Hans about his family, his eyes filled with tears and he could only shake his head and shrug helplessly. Evidently, they had a small shop in a German village which the Nazis trashed, taking his father, mother, and sister away somewhere. That was when Hans managed to sneak onto a train to Basel and then come to Milan. He met Franco through his community and Harriet took him to the American Embassy and helped him apply for a visa to safety in the states.

Only after the visa was granted did we learn about Franco and Harriet's role in Hans' bid for freedom. However, we noticed in retrospect that Hans' visits always coincided with Linda's day off.

Our part of the conversation was mostly answering his questions. He wanted to know how much it would cost him to stay in New York and other difficult to answer questions. Last time we saw him, he seemed to be vibrating with excitement. His visa had been accepted and he was leaving in two days. We were so happy for him and asked that he write to us when he was settled. Incredibly, in just a couple of months we received a letter from him from St. Louis. He had gotten a job with a company there. He even had his name on the letterhead. America was still the land of opportunity.

There was one last anecdote about Hans which we learned from him in later years. When he finally landed in New York he felt thirsty so he went into a drugstore to find a drink—perhaps a soda. There was a counter where ice cream was being served, but since it was his first time, he had no idea what to order. Looking around he saw an advertisement on the wall that had a large color photo of a glass of bubbling liquid, so he ordered that, drank it down, and asked for another. Once he got settled and made friends, he told them about his first thirst quencher in America. It turned out he had enjoyed two full glasses of Alka-Seltzer!

Rose

The life I was leading was so different and filled with such interesting people that I sometimes had to remind myself that I was still Becky Fahrig from Joplin. We heard very little daily news from America and the propensity of youth to live in the present was exaggerated for me. There was no past and the future was only tomorrow. I loved each moment and looked at the constant stream of people we were meeting and wondered about their lives. Mine was almost a dream.

Lots of American women in Milan were married to Italian men. I can remember one time being at a large party. I was sitting with Rose Barsotti who was married to an Italian Army officer. Rose was that young, dark-haired beauty from Alabama whom I knew through the Club. She had been there only two years. We had become close friends, being the same age, and she was pointing out to me a charming lady across the room.

"She is American and has been living in Italy 30 years," Rose whispered.

Looking again at the woman, I felt a kind of pity rise in my heart and I thought, "How could this be? Who would want to stay away from one's own country for so long? I knew I wouldn't." I turned and saw in Rose's eyes the same feeling.

Of course, my dear sister, Harriet would be another life-long expat, living over sixty years in Milan and later in nearby Bergamo. But that part of her story was hidden far over the horizon in the future out of the sight of we young women. Dear, sweet Rose wouldn't stay long. We could not know then that war would soon send her and her son back to Alabama and claim the life of her young husband. But tonight, how good that we could gossip and laugh and not be afraid.

Venice

Franco and Harriet had finally settled on a villa for the summer in a little village on Lake Maggiore. We would be there for July and August and since May was upon us, Harriet said we better see Venice before it got too hot.

"Oh dear," she mused. "The next two weeks are full. Let's go the 18th, then Franco can go with us."

We took the train at 6 a.m. and bought second class seats for the three of us and Franco, who had a yearly pass because he traveled so much, rode in first class. I had thought Harriet was trying to cut our expenses, but it turned out otherwise. First class had plush, upholstered seats, second class, only wooden benches. When the conductor came through Harriet noticed an attitude of scorn as he commented. "Isn't that your husband up in first class.?" When he left Harriet laughed and told us that a lot of women didn't like to ride first class because sometimes the plush seats had fleas. That's why she and the babies always rode on the benches. Evidently the men were used to the fleas!

The train stopped for a minute in Padua where Franco's older brother Mario and his wife Giselda lived. Giselda was at the station to say hello and meet Blossom and me. She was going to join us in Venice for the day. I had always thought Venice was a coastal city with the sea running into it. How surprised I was to find it actually situated two miles out into the Adriatic Sea. It covered nearly 100 islands with 400 bridges connecting them.

Giselda was a pleasant, matronly woman about 40 years old who spoke no English. We muddled along with our minimal language skills, Harriet translating when necessary until we crossed a long bridge and reached the station in Venice. Then we experienced the glory of riding in a gondola down the Grand Canal.

I loved Venice from the start. We settled into a small hotel and walked to Piazza San Marco. It is an enormous rectangular square with St.

Marks church at one end. The other three sides were lined with shops, businesses and restaurants with tables and chairs out in the open. We sat there drinking café latte and enjoying the fabulous scene – the bright blue weather, the ancient buildings, the people, the pigeons. Franco told us that this square was called 'the drawing room of Europe.' With Harriet and Franco as our hosts, we saw it as an elaborate, marble-floored extension of their gracious apartment on Via Sidoli in Milan.

Harriet, of course, was the ideal tour guide, taking us around this city built largely during the crusades in the tenth, eleventh and twelfth centuries. It is sort of the museum of the Mediterranean. First, to give their city the necessary gravitas and attract the holy worshippers, they stole the body of the apostle St. Mark from its original burial site across the sea in Alexandria, Egypt. That let them name their new cathedral St. Marks. The Lion is the symbol of St. Mark, and therefore of the city of Venice.

The four magnificent bronze horses which grace the facade of the cathedral, were captured by the crusaders in Constantinople. Inside, the cathedral glitters with golden walls and ceilings all covered with gilded mosaic tiles. It gives the impression of walking into a magnificent piece of jewelry.

Then there was a long Gondola ride and a visit to Franco's other brother Claudio and his wife Nelsa who lived and worked on the nearby island of Murano. This is the center of the famous glass foundries where lovely and elaborate glassworks are blown. Claudio is a photographer of fine art and one of the few allowed into the great museums of Europe with his camera. In later years his photographs would be reproduced in the large Abrams art books on our coffee tables. We were in Venice only two days but we saw wonders in that short time.

On the way back we stopped in Padua to visit Mario and Giselda. Mario was darling, an artist of great talent. A sister named Titania completed Franco's family.

Harriet and Franco left us there for two days as they returned to Milan. We had to speak Italian as no one that we met in Padua spoke English. Mario and Giselda invited their good friends Ezio and Roberto and their girlfriends Adele and Lucy over to meet us. These two men were delightfully entertaining. I can't remember what they did for a living, but they could have been clowns or comedians. Since we had such a language barrier, they put on an impromptu pantomime for our entertainment. For two days, they kept us in stitches as they showed us around Padua. We took some pictures of them clowning and imitating the German tourists.

We had a wonderful time and adored the food. Giselda made polenta, corn meal cooked in a large bowl until it has the consistency of a jelled pudding, then turned out on a large wooden platter. She cut it with a string drawn through it and served it with tender veal and lots of gravy covering the polenta. They had a few friends in for dinner and Mario made place cards by drawing a small caricature of each of us.

Back on a train to Milan we found ourselves in a car full of Italians, mostly soldiers. They were very friendly and when I got cold one of the officers gallantly put his cape around me. Blossom and I, in our conversations, must have mentioned Milan. Although they didn't speak English, one of the men caught that word and asked us if we were going to Milan.

"Yes, why?"

"Because" he said, "this train is going to Paris."

"Oh MY GOSH!" and we burst out laughing at this ridiculous situation. "What can we do?" we asked.

These kind men talked among themselves and with great excitement pointed out the window. Then to our surprise one of them reached up, pulled the heavy cord which stopped the train. We looked out and saw that we were in the middle of nowhere. The conductor came in to see what the matter was. Everyone started talking at once and pointing to us. An unsettling feeling came over me.

They talked too fast for us to understand it all, but we got the idea we were to get off the train. The conductor was a kind old gentleman who helped us off on the right side of the train and pointed back to a little waiting shelter about a block behind us. He took out his pocket watch and ran his finger around the dial one time, meaning an hour and a train would come and pick us up. Somehow, we asked him, "How would that train know to stop?"

"I will tell them," he assured us.

We had a sinking feeling as the train chugged off leaving us standing with our suitcases in the middle of a field. We walked back to the little shelter and sat down. As the hour neared for the train to come, we tried to stay calm. We looked around and wondered if we were in Switzerland? How far had we traveled from Padua? Were those distant mountains the Alps? At last we heard the train approach. Would it stop? We waved and shouted like the desperate Americans we were, and whether our antics or the conductor's promise—something caused the train to grind to a steamy, squealing stop. We had rehearsed our question for the new conductor who opened his door for us.

"A Milano? A Milano?"

"Si, si," he nodded as though he was merely confirming the obvious. "Yes, you frantic Americanatas," he seemed to say, "the sky is still overhead."

We plopped our suitcases down and breathed the sighs of people who are no longer accidentally on their way to Paris.

Thank God.

Denis

Back in Milan, we picked up again on the teas and dinners, either at our house or friends. Jeff called often and one day he asked Blossom and me to a dinner with English friends.

May 27th would become a date that changed my life in Italy, and in a way, Blossom's too. I can't remember what the occasion was, but Jeff had told us we were 'dressing' for dinner, which meant formal gowns for us, tuxes for the men.

Because the day was unusually chilly, I wore the coat Mother had given me for Christmas. It was a long black velvet evening wrap with puffed sleeves and a white fur collar. Gardenias were in bloom, so I tucked one in my hair. I felt quite dressed up and so did Blossom who was wearing her gray fur jacket. Mac and Jeff picked us up in a cab and we went first to the Wright's, a youngish English couple. When we arrived the rest of the guests were already there. Lockhead and Dorothy Shaw, the Wrights, a Jane somebody who was Mac's date and a handsome young man with dark curly hair, brown eyes, and a ready smile. Jeff stepped forward to introduce us: "Becky Fahrig, meet Denis Passadoro." We shook hands and our eyes met in that direct sort of 'recognizing' way—here was someone special.

I thought, "Where has he been all this time?"

He told me later that he was thinking, "I'll bet she is expensive." For an unsophisticated girl from Missouri that was the ultimate compliment.

"Lovely to meet you ... Becky...? is that right?"

"Yes, Becky—short for Rebecca."

"And Becky Fahrig..."

"Yes..."

"But you're American, not German..."

"That's right. And I'm not Jewish either... And you are Mr. Passa...?"

"Passadoro—but you must call me Denis."

"Denis Passadoro."

"Right"

"And you are British, not Italian...?"

"Right. My Grandfather Passadoro emigrated years ago..."

"Just as my Grandfather Fahrig did!"

"A pair of lovely old gentlemen, I'm sure.

"They might've been friends if only they had met..."

"Thank goodness we have managed to..."

"At last!"

"Yes, friends at last!"

We laughed and shook hands again.

Denis sat across from me and many times when I looked at him, I found his eyes on me. I was so taken with his looks. He was exceedingly

handsome with dark hair, smooth face, slight build, about five foot ten, eyes fringed with thick lashes any girl would die for. Who did he remind me of? Oh yes, he looked like a young Charles Boyer the French movie star. He was 29 years old. I found him deeply attractive. It was a new and exhilarating experience for me to be so taken with a man rather than the boys I had grown used to.

The next morning Denis called and invited Blossom and me to dinner at his house. He quickly called again and asked if we would mind "dressing?" At home we would say "dressing formally." Here it was just 'dressing.' I loved it.

This Hollywood fantasy trip was beginning to feel very personal. I hoped I could maintain it.

Jeff picked us up in a cab. There were only six of us in the party, Lockhead and Dorothy, Jeff and Denis and the two of us. Denis' apartment was large and masculine with comfortable leather furniture and formal dining room. In the living room was a large painting of a dog listening at the horn from an old-fashioned phonograph. Both Blossom and I recognized it as the symbol of the RCA company and commented about it. "Yes," Denis said, "that is the original painting. It's called "His Master's Voice." You see, my uncle was one of the founders of RCA, and I work for RCA."

Jeff spoke up. "Denis is head of RCA for all of Italy, and every musician is always glad to have him in the audience".

"It's a lovely painting and reminds me of my childhood," I told him. "My grandmother Short had just such a phonograph with a large purple cone, and it played recordings with a wooden needle."

Dinner was served by his housekeeper-cook and was excellent. As all meals seem to be in Europe, it was served in courses with many utensils on each side and above the plate. We watched Denis closely for cues and saved ourselves any embarrassment. I wondered if this might have been the original reason to always wait for the host or hostess to take the first bite.

Using a fish knife, which was placed above the plate, was another new experience for me. I also found it interesting that the delicious bread, a hard dinner roll, was simply set on the tablecloth without a plate beneath it. Thereafter, I noticed that in paintings of Italian dinner scenes going back to the Renaissance, the bread was depicted in just this way. It was a wonderful meal of soup, fish, pasta, lamb, salad, fruit and dessert.

Afterwards we went to the Vecchio Milano for music and dancing. It was quickly apparent that Denis was my date and Jeff was Blossom's. That suited me to a T.

As we descended the stairs with the large mirror on the landing, I glimpsed our reflection and caught my breath. We looked so happy! There we were arrayed in our finest, laughing, young and as beautiful as we would ever be. I would have liked to stop and savor that moment, but we continued on with the laughter of the others behind us into that lovely room filled with music. The image of us on that staircase, the pleasure of that moment in my memory, is one I will always treasure.

As we were seated, I noticed the band leader nod to Denis who waved back. What a good time we were having, A Saturday night to remember forever.

"I loved your apartment," I said when our drinks were delivered.

"It's too often lonely," he said. "What have you seen since arriving ...when was it?"

"February 6th. We've seen Rome, Florence, Venice and a field three miles past Verona," I replied.

"Beg pardon?"

And I told him about the interrupted train ride to Paris.

"Well, I figured you would stop traffic," he laughed, "but the trains as well?"

Everyone around the table laughed. I felt grateful for the compliment but more than that, I felt the privilege of being paired off with this man whom all his smart friends so admired. His intelligence and wit had been on display all evening and I was realizing for the first time in my young life that there was such a thing as leadership on the social scale. Denis was one of those people who, naturally and seemingly without effort stepped forward and took the lead in conversation. All of us around the table seemed to lean toward him and hang on his every word.

We danced and talked with that special feeling you have when you are getting to know a new friend. We were a wonderful, happy group and when we left, we all knew we would do this again. Denis and Jeff took us home in Denis' Alfa Romeo. It was very late, but he drove slowly, pulling me over to him as he drove. A good night kiss and I was in heaven.

The Two of Us

The next day was Sunday. We spent the day with Harriet and Franco and in the afternoon, we watched a religious parade and ceremony in the street below. The large church just across the street was always interesting to us. On special days – and there were many – the church was completely draped in fabric, a different color depending on the celebration. Red when a Cardinal was coming, white for a wedding, black for a funeral. The music, the priest and acolytes carrying crosses and statues, waving censors and blessing the crowd—all this was a source of wonder to us, ignorant American Protestants that we were.

That night Denis called and set up another dinner with the same group for the next evening. We went to the Piccolo Bar for cocktails, Tantals for dinner and the Odeon to dance. I was astonished at the scope and variety of the nightlife in Milan. Are all cities this busy after midnight? It's really a question in retrospect—at the time I simply dove in and loved all these new experiences.

As Denis and I were dancing he said to me, "I must go on a short business trip Wednesday. I had planned to leave tomorrow evening, but I want to see you again. So instead of taking the train tomorrow, I will wait until Wednesday morning and fly. Let's have lunch and dinner together tomorrow, just the two of us."

Our day together was the best. The weather was perfect, one of those warm sunny days that late May can bring. After lunch at Gianino's we sauntered along the avenue stopping at one of the many flower stalls in Milan and Denis bought me a huge bunch of red carnations; there must have been five dozen! I had been sent flowers before, but never had I stood with a man, and a beautiful, charming man at that, and had him buy me such an array. I could hardly believe this was happening to me. I simply loved being with Denis.

For dinner we drove in his red Alpha Romeo out of town and stopped at a charming little country inn. We took a long ride afterward, visiting and talking and getting better acquainted. He was an only child, his father had passed away, their family home was on the outskirts of London. He loved sailing and had a sailboat in England. When we stopped by his apartment for a short hour, he showed me pictures of his home, a handsome, Georgian style building, and beautiful sailboat that I learned was a sloop. He loved music and his work. While we were at his apartment, he took me in his arms and told me that he loved me.

More thoughts in retrospect...this was moving awfully fast. But at twenty everything seems to be racing along at sixty miles an hour. I remembered kissing Larry on the ship and becoming 'Ann' for an evening with him. Would Denis fade away like he did? But Larry was a kid, and Denis is a man—and a very different sort of person. This must be all part of the education of travel that our dear mother told us about. Stop worrying and enjoy it I thought...and inside I shrugged my shoulders, and I kissed him deeply and said I loved him, too. What the heck.

And then he took me home.

With Denis in Rome for ten days, I had time to think about and react to the past week's events. The reaction came in the form of a letdown and a cold. Was I caring too much? My mind was in a whirl. How much did he really care? I felt quite vulnerable. With Denis gone so long I was plagued by sudden doubts. I languished in bed with my cold and my anxiety.

This gave Jeff and Blossom time to be together, which is what they wanted all along. He had always been so gallant to include both of us and had come to visit the family. Since he had started out with me at our lovely lunch in the Galleria, I could see that he had shifted his interest to my sister. Plus, we always had our 'mountain-climber-conferences' where we worked out our feelings with each other and managed to avoid falling into the dangerous abysses.

He and Blossom developed a warm and caring relationship. He called her, "My wee pest," and she called him, "Ya big galoot." And they both laughed.

Jeff was the vice president in Italy representing the J. and P. Coats Thread Company. He was the "salt of the earth" type of fellow, kind and genuine, with his charming Scottish burr and a good sense of humor. He and Blossom went out several times that week while I was nursing my cold. Finally, our conference decided, "Hey, this is Italy! Let's have love affairs! What the heck!"

Denis came back from Rome on June 10th. He picked me up and we drove to a park with trees in full bloom. They reminded me so of the apple trees at Lord's Orchard when I was a child.

"Darling, we have to talk," I told him the tears beginning.

"Yes, we do," he said, taking my hand.

"I've been frightened..."

"I can imagine..." he said.

"This is all so new..."

"Yes, it is and I'm sorry if I frightened you."

"Well, you did! I mean you do..." I had to get away from him. I jumped out and walked toward the lake...he followed.

"Its good that we're talking about it..." he said.

"You need to understand..." tears and sobs.

He embraced me from behind, putting his face near mine.

"I'm sorry, darling, but I think I do understand..."

"Can't we just slow down and talk about it...?" I turned and embraced him back.

"I want that too," he said.

And so, we did talk there with the beautiful trees and the lovely blue lake. I told him how small and alone I felt even with my sisters near. And how I'd never felt love for a man like I felt for him and how scared I was to really believe it because he seemed too perfect. So maybe he was only some fantasy like I had as a child. And all the time I was telling him these things, he was hugging me and telling me "It's okay, it's okay" but I wasn't listening to him yet, because I still had more fear to tell. So, then he kissed me and I said, "Can we get back in the car now?" Because I felt exposed out here in the open.

So, he led me to the car and I asked him to put the top up, please, because I wanted to feel safer—so, after the top was up and the windows rolled up too, I took a deep breath and let out a sigh...

"Is it about making love?" he asked me, gently.

And again the tears—"I'm so afraid."

"Of course, you are...so am I." He was looking at me directly now, with a small smile and raised eyebrows. I felt his honesty and caring coming to me.

"You are?"

"Absolutely. It's the truest, most dangerous thing that can happen between two people. It scares everybody, and it should!"

"It does?"

"Without doubt." He reached and took my hand. "So, it should not happen casually. Save that enormous event for your wedding night."

"Oh, Denis..." and the tears came again, but this time with a huge feeling of relief.

"Here's my proposal," he said touching my face gently, "You are on holiday, right?"

"Yes, indeed!"

"Italy was created just for holiday!" His voice rose with excitement.

I caught his tone of joy and joined in, "The whole world is a holiday!"

"That's the spirit!" Denis laughed, "so come on! There's work to do!"

"And Play!"

"Especially, PLAY!"

We were both grinning like fools and Denis said, "Can I put the top down now?"

"Yes, let's go Play!" I was so relieved. Our conversation had erased my fears and I couldn't wait to share it with my sister.

We opened the red car up and motored through the streets of Italy—fearlessly!

Lugano

In the next week, my diary tells me I saw him every day. We either went to dinner or he came to the apartment for a visit. Sometimes we took in a show. Memory is fickle and most of the details on these dates are a blur to me now, but a few events stand out. The four of us, Jeff, Denis, Blossom, and I embarked upon outings that continued, off and on all summer. Too much time has elapsed to remember details, but the feelings are still fresh and vivid in my heart.

June brings ideal weather to Switzerland and we made the most of it. Leaving Milan at 9 a.m. we drove north for about 50 miles till we reached Lake Lugano. On the map, it seems as if Switzerland reaches out a friendly, welcoming hand and shares some of its beautiful alpine foothills with its next-door neighbor. There, within easy reach of Milan, is a splendid lake and a sweet Swiss village both named 'Lugano'.

On the near shore we came to a dear little place called the Chateau de San Georgio. It sat right on the lake and was a darling little rustic-looking building with a café and rooms to dress for swimming. Outside under giant shade trees and weeping willows were tables and chairs. There was a dock of sorts with a diving board over the lake. Blossom and I were simply enchanted with the whole scene and bubbled with enthusiasm. The men became infected by high spirits as well, and we spent a good deal of our time in a state of giddy euphoria.

The owner was a plump, cheerful, Swiss woman who brought mugs of coffee and hot, homemade coffee cake without our even asking. Could it get any better than this? We doubted it. Would we be here for lunch? "Si! Certo!" Perfect!

As we sat talking and learning more about each other's' backgrounds, some of our biggest laughs were over the language we all spoke. They, being British, used such terms as the 'bonnet' on the car, the 'lift' in the apartment. When Jeff mentioned that his aunt did 'croshette' we were lost.

"What is croshette?"

He said, "You know, with a hook, like this," working his fingers.

Blossom said, "You mean crochet!"

We all got the giggles at the four English-speaking people who couldn't understand each other.

Finally, Denis said, "Maybe we'd be better off speaking Italian," which brought even more howls. One recent event underscored this particular limitation.

The week before we were eating out together. Our waiter spoke no English and I was trying to use as much Italian as I could. I had pretty good luck discovering cognates—taking an English word and giving it an Italian ending. 'Timid,' for instance—one just added 'a' and said 'timida'(tee-mee⊠-da). It worked!

Well, at dinner on this particular evening I got brave and made up a word for the fruit course. I ordered figs. Denis choked on his drink, Jeff let out a whistle and the waiter made a quick exit. I realized I had goofed and teetered on the brink of extreme embarrassment. Thank goodness everyone laughed.

"Becky, you probably don't even know that word in English," said Denis. Now under the willow trees we laughed all over again.

The sun was warm, and we put on our suits and got in the lake. What a delicious feeling it was to be in this place at this time. The water was clear and cool, the low foothills to the Alps rimmed the far side of the lake, villages tucked close to the water, their white buildings shining in the sun, and now and then a church bell tolling the hour. We frolicked like children. We looked at Jeff and Denis as they splashed water on each other like small boys.

"They are having as much fun as we are," we said to one another.

Blossom and I practiced diving, something we had done all our lives, not realizing the fellows had gone in the chalet, ordered lunch and brought out big fluffy snow-white towels. When I got back to the table, Denis got behind me and wrapped one of these towels around me. To my surprise the towel reached from my ears to my ankles. As he tucked it under my chin his mouth close to my ear he whispered, "I love you," and I whispered back. We never made much display of emotion, for at that time it was improper and besides we were quite reserved. Normally.

We sat at the table in the little grove of willows and laughed at Jeff trying to get the towel around Blossom. She was so small, only five-foot two, and the towel so wide Jeff had to bunch it around her neck. He was tall and big framed. Together they were a real Mutt and Jeff; no pun intended. Jeff called Blossom a "Wee Pest" always with affection and his twinkling smile. Then he put his towel around his head in sheik fashion, put his arm out – leaned against a tree and announced his pleasure in the day.

Blossom

As we ate lunch of pasta, salad, bread and wine, we continued the discussion of our enjoyment. Just who said what is immaterial, but it went something like this.

"Together we are the best company."

"That's it. We ARE a company."

"No, we are the Board of Directors of the company."

"Of course, and what is the name of this English-American Company?"

"How about Hot Times?"

"How about Hot Lips, Ltd?"

"YES!"

"All in favor?"

"YES!"

Then Jeff said, "And the first order of business is to plan for the fudge party you girls have promised us. I hereby start it off by commandeering these three wee packets of sugar towards the fudge."

"And," added Denis, "we will only use sugar taken when we have dined together."

The Senora came out with dessert, warm apple strudel. A far-off bell told us it was one o'clock, and we still had lots to look forward to. We would cross the lake and drive to the village of Lugano on the other side. We would look in shops, buy trinkets, be lazy at outdoor tables all the while enjoying the pots of flowers and mini gardens scattered along the wide avenue that fronted the lake. On the

Jeff

lake side of this street benches sitting on lush green grass would be the perfect place for us to sit and watch the moon rise. The end of a perfect day. But no, not the end, for we would go back to Denis' apartment and cook bacon and eggs.

The next day Denis called to say his mother was arriving for a ten-day visit and he wouldn't be able to spend much time with me. We sisters went to the British/American wives Club which was the last one for the season. That evening Franco danced with Blossom and me in the marble foyer to music from the radio; he was a wonderful dancer. Although we had long talks on the phone, I didn't see Denis for five days.

Blossom had gone out with Jeff and added to the sugar supply so when Denis called at last and said he was free, "Could we go to dinner and maybe get the final bit of sugar to make fudge?" This we did, eating at Maggalino's. I asked about his mother and he said she had a head-ache and retired early.

He had obviously told her about me because he said, "Mother told me to remember American girls are spoiled."

I thought "She's afraid of me."

We took our sugar home and sure enough we had plenty for the fudge. Jeff and Mac were there, and Harriet supervised. It turned into candy-making party with all six of us pitching in and telling jokes. Our fudge recipe worked just as it had in Joplin. Denis left around 10:30 taking a sample for his mother. It was delicious.

His Mother

One day after his mother came, Denis asked us for tea to meet her. Although their name is Passadoro, which was his Italian great grandfather's name, Denis and his mother are very British, especially his mother. She was fair skinned with light hair flecked with just a touch of grey, not at all like Denis's dark hair. She was pleasant and motherly toward Denis, who tried not to be nervous. Blossom talked on easily while I tried to forget that she thought we American girls were spoiled. I didn't help my cause any when somewhere in the conversation I referred to "the cleaning lady." The minute I said it I knew it was a blunder. The British never use the word 'lady' with anyone who is not an aristocratic "Lady." She stiffened and I could feel myself sinking under her metallic blue gaze.

The following day, Blossom and I went with Denis and his mother up to the little Chalet San Giorgio. I think he wanted his mother to get better acquainted with me, but the day fell pretty flat. It was difficult to recapture the giddy euphoria we had shared swimming and lunching under the willows with the chilly Mrs. Passadoro looking on. I was relieved when the late afternoon arrived and we were dropped back at the warmth of Harriet and Franco's apartment. A quick hug from the little boys and the stiffness of the day was forgotten.

The day ended on a brighter note. In the evening we went to a party at the Winfield's. It is always fun to go with Harriet and Franco whose friends have large, elegant parties. This evening had a good mix of English, American and Italian with quite a few people who were new to us. These parties sometimes would last until two, three or four in the morning. Of course, they started late, never before 8:00 and often 9 or 9:30. It wasn't a dinner party—we weren't there to eat, but drink.

I was getting pretty good at making a drink last a long time. There was always a lot of drinking, but no one ever seemed to have too much.

This particular evening the only thing they seemed to be serving was wine. I knew it was champagne because of the bubbles from the bottom of the stem, so it didn't bother me when I was given another one. I had just finished that when someone proposed a toast. I found myself with a fresh glass and drank to the toast.

All seemed well. Then I heard my name called. I turned around and found Mrs. Anderson and her friend, two English ladies that I liked very much, sitting on the sofa across the room. I walked closer to be able to hear what they were saying to me. Mrs. Anderson wanted me to come to a children's party. I stood there in front of that sofa, looking at her and suddenly I was shocked to see two Mrs. Andersons!

I accepted the invitation, and thanked the Mrs. Anderson on the left, with some small doubt that she was the authentic Mrs. Anderson. Excusing myself, I moved out to the balcony. I didn't feel lightheaded, nor dizzy...was I drunk? A few minutes in the cool night air and it passed.

On the way home Franco commented that the champagne cocktails were pretty strong. No wonder, I was tipsy. I resolved to guard against that happening again. In a way, that experience was a blessing in disguise for from that time on I watched what I drank. I have never liked the feeling of not being in complete control.

The Opera

By tradition, in late June, La Scala, the world renown opera house of Milan, staged a few operas in the open courtyard of the Sforza castle. The Sforza's were the powerful family who ruled the city in the 1400s and their castle, smack in the center of the city, is immense. Harriet announced that Aida was playing, and we should go. The day was warm and pleasant, so we were assured of a fine evening. Denis called and wanted us to have dinner with him and his mother, but because of our plans we had to decline. We were had to stand in line to get tickets, so arriving early was imperative. We had a good-sized snack in the late afternoon and went to the castle two hours ahead of time. There was already a long line of people, but it didn't discourage us. We got good seats and were simply awed by the size of the courtyard.

The setting for Aida is Egypt and it was spectacular. Everything was on a huge scale – the most magnificent production beyond what I expected, though Harriet told me Aida is often a big deal. On the grand entrance of Radames coming home from war, no circus has had a more impressive procession. There were tigers, and three or four elephants, hundreds of extras, and of course the marvelous music of Verdi.

The very next night we went back again to the castle to see La Boheme by Puccini. Again, Denis called and wanted us to join him at the opera but since Harriet, Blossom and I were going as well, we said we'd see him there. For two acts Blossom changed places with Denis and sat with his mother so he and I could sit together. What a dear sister. Opera had become an important new experience for me. First of all, we were in the country where these composers lived, and their music seemed to grow right out of the landscape. Then, we were sitting in a castle which they would have known, amid an audience of their countrymen and women. I was too green to know any of the singers, but their voices were splendid. While I had little idea of the words, the music evoked such feelings that I sometimes found tears in my eyes without quite knowing why.

Harriet was a great lover of all music, but where opera was concerned, she is what's known as an 'aficionado'. I asked her how she came to be that way and she told me that our mother taught her when Harriet began learning to play the piano. This came as a surprise to me, as being the last in line, I had missed so much of my sibling's childhood lessons. I was hungry to learn about what mother had taught, and Harriet could see I felt a bit left out, so we had a long talk one evening.

I learned that Mama, who our family had always described as, "Born in Superior, with a Superior mind" was more than just 'smart', as I could see for myself, but she had a truly remarkable intelligence. This manifested itself in her musical mind. Florence Short Fahrig was a bit of a prodigy as a child, learning the piano quite young, like Harriet. I realized that must be the source of a barrier between Mama and me. I had never been drawn to the piano and disliked the long, tedious hours of practice that were necessary for me to master even the simple Bach Minuet that I could play. But Mama and now I realized Harriet as well, were both wonderful at the keyboard! They tossed off whole pages of the Russian masters—Tchaikovsky and Rachmaninoff with gusto! Harriet could even turn them into polkas on her accordion!

I remember mother making a speech at one of her DAR meetings usually held at the Masonic Temple. Some years Blossom and I would dress up like George and Martha Washington—since I was the younger of us, I was Martha at first, but in time I towered over my sister by an inch or two and I got to wear the knee britches and tri-corner hat. Mother sometimes spoke about opera in those speeches, and I recall her mentioning the time she got to see the Great Caruso sing at the Met in New York.

Now, even though grand opera was not really my cup of tea, and even less so for Blossom, we understood the importance of this event for those we loved and were glad to share it with them. Of course, Harriet was the perfect guide, and Denis too, explaining the story and holding my hand. I look back on it now with gratitude that I was able to experience such an evening. There I sat under a warm Italian night filled with stars and magnificent music—twenty-one, holding hands with a man who loved me, hearing La Boheme for the first time. Wouldn't it become your favorite opera, too?

Summer

By now it was getting close to the time we would move to the villa in the country for the summer. Denis's mother left, and he and I had a couple more dinner dates. On July first we drove out into the country where we had gone before. There was a little trattoria with tables in the garden. Jasmin and other fragrances filled the soft Italian evening. As we ate and enjoyed the balmy night, he told me a great deal about England.

"Do you miss it?" I asked him.

"Yes, I suppose I do," he answered. "Of course, I couldn't wish myself anyplace else than here with you right now." He always said such sweet, thoughtful things.

"Nor I," I told him, taking his hand across the table.

"And you?" he asked. "Don't you miss Joplin, Missouri?"

"I do have pangs of homesickness from time to time, but they aren't lasting. Italy is like a dream and I don't want to wake up ..." We smiled at each other tenderly. "Besides, I know I will be going back home in a few months."

"So will I, I'm afraid."

"Why afraid?"

"It looks like Europe is sliding toward a nasty patch."

"You think there will be a war?" I asked.

"I'm pretty sure of it." He squeezed my hand. It was the first time he had spoken of war, and even then, he would not utter the word. We steered our talk to happier things—the food, the flowers around us, the music drifting out from a radio in the kitchen. The radio turned to a news broadcast about Hitler and Mussolini and as if by a chilly breeze, the candle of our happy evening was blown out.

Denis' face was suddenly dark with emotion. My heart went cold.

"If war comes, must you fight?" I asked.

"You saw that Fascist in Rome," he said stressing the word Fascist. "Did he strike you as a peace-loving leader?"

I had to admit not and shook my head.

"The truth is, for all his strutting bluster, he's a weak man," Denis said through gritted teeth. "And there's nothing more dangerous than a weak man with an army."

"What will you do?" I asked, knowing the answer.

"As I love my country, I have my duty," he replied with a smile.

The music came back on the radio. it was Benny Goodman's band playing 'Begin the Beguine'. Denis took my hand and stood up. I stood too. Suddenly he embraced me and very slowly he began to dance with me in his arms. It wasn't a dance floor, only a terrace with smooth, flat stones. There may have been other people at the tables but we didn't pay them any attention. The music swelled and we danced until it ended. We kissed. He stepped back, still holding my hand, and with a smile and a relaxed wave of his hand—he spoke: "As Robert Louis Stevenson said, 'There is no duty we so much underrate as the duty of being happy.'"

We walked back to his Alfa Romeo and he said, "Tonight there is no duty for me but happiness."

Weekend at Lugano

The following day, a Friday, Harriet, Franco, Linda, and the little boys, all left for Maccagno. They got away about 11 o'clock in the morning. I dressed and met Denis at his office where I helped him with a list of records he had to finish by Saturday. We lunched at his apartment, and we then picked up Jeff and went to get Blossom for a day's outing. We discussed the possibility of Denis and Jeff taking us up to Maccagno the next day.

Suddenly Denis said, "I have a smashing idea. Why don't we just pack everything and not come back tonight? We could go for the weekend and end up at Maccagno tomorrow?"

To go away with two men for the weekend was a rash thing for us to do. But who would know? So, we held a meeting of the 'Board of Directors' and the vote was unanimous.

"Let's do it!".

We scurried to get all our things, packed an overnight bag, stopped by the men's apartments and got their bags. Laughter, excitement.

"Don't forget to lock the door!"

"What will people think?"

"They will never know."

Coming down the stairs in this dither of exhilaration, I dropped my little vanity case. It burst open like a pinata, and a thousand and one little personal items went flying all over the steps and through the open risers to the floor below. The entire arsenal of feminine allure lay scattered across yards of Italian tile. There were pins - bobby, safety, straight, hat; little bottles and jars - fragrances, creams, deodorants, ointments; tubes of lipstick and toothpaste; make-up, rouges, foundation; brushes, combs, tweezers. All the cosmetics and implements that a woman requires and denies that she requires. I was mortified. Why was I always making a "bruta figura"?

"Jackpot!" Denis called out, as though I had hit plums on a slot machine.

That saved me and we all laughed and began the task of gathering.

Of course, they all helped pick up, with a few funny remarks from the men, especially when Jeff picked up my eyelash curler and remarked having seen the same thing among the instruments of torture at the Tower of London. At length we were off. We held a board meeting to decide where to go. It was easy to choose Lugano. We had tea on the way at Castello Puro, one of the many charming places to stop along the lake.

When we arrived in Lugano the men chose the Hotel du Lac, a very large hotel that had a minimum of intimacy. Our rooms were on the same floor but Jeff and Denis's room was a long way down the hall from Blossom's and mine. We had a late dinner at the hotel and then hit the night spots, not getting to bed until 4:30. In spite of the late night, we were up at 9:30 and all went for a swim followed by ham and eggs and wonderful Swiss coffeecake. We took our time driving to the Villa at Maccagno getting there just in time for lunch which was, per force, simple. It was good to see the family and find the villa delightfully spacious.

Maccagno

Blossom and I had a lovely bedroom to ourselves, a relief from the living room sofas in Milan. There was a large lawn and garden area. A garden wall separated the house from the little gravel road. After lunch we took a walk and found a bocci court and had a rousing game.

It was after dinner that Denis brought out his surprise. Before he opened it, he made a little speech. "As you know this is the 3rd of July, the eve of the 4th and it calls for a celebration." Blossom and I thought how nice for him to remember our Independence Day. Denis continued, "So I have with me some fireworks that we may celebrate England getting rid of those bothersome colonies." We whooped and hollered and argued history, but all agreed it had a happy ending. The fireworks were the final touch before they left for Milan that night.

Maccagno was a small village tucked in the foothills of the Alps and right on the shore of Lake Maggiore, so named because it is the largest of the Italian Lakes. The town is actually named Maccagno Inferiore as opposed to Maccagno Superiore which is the village further up the mountain. Our villa was just a short walk from the town square and in the other direction, equally distant, was the river and its entrance to the lake.

The villa itself was a large two-story stucco house with tall, wide, casement windows. As there are no flies or mosquitos here, there were no screens, only shutters that rolled down to shut out the light or the elements. It was quite close to the road, and from the front upstairs windows we could see the lake which sparkled in the sun. Inside our bedroom we could pull on the heavy cord that raised the roller blinds and hang out the window to survey our domain. This would be our home for the next two months.

The little boys were with us in our room "helping" put things away and playing in the boxes. The windows were open. When we had things fairly well organized, we said "Basta! Let's get outside." Scooping Frankie up in my arms, with Blossom and Dickie running ahead of us, we ran out into the garden. After a few games of Ring-Around-the-Rosies, Dickie saw two chairs that happened to be in a row.

"Let's play train!" he chirped.

We pushed several other chairs together and all got in for a train ride. When Linda called "Mangia!" (Come eat!), we started in. On the way, we noticed a huge hydrangea growing against the wall. The flowers were almost as big as Frankie's head. Blossom ran in and got the camera while I stood Frankie next to the flower to have his picture taken. It is a dear little snapshot; the flower is just a bit shorter than the child.

The days were warm and lazy in this out of the way place. It was as if we had stepped back in time. Blossom and I wore shorts and halter tops to catch the sun as we walked to the little shops that make up this tiny village. The weather was glorious! The road leading up to Maccagno Superiore rose along the side of the hill was an easy slope which we hiked to the shop that sells yarn. We both had knitting projects going and had grown passionate for their beautiful soft wools.

Walking back down this road with our new yarn, we noticed an old woman carrying a tall wicker basket, apparently filled with hay or straw, strapped to her back. She looked old but it was hard to tell. She was dressed all in black, as were most of the village women between thirty and ninety. Her basket was packed solid and high over the rim and must have been heavy. She was bent over and her hands were busy with some knitting. She glanced at us and then it seemed she was starting to have some sort of fit. I heard her screaming "Americanata" and some word I did not know and spitting on the ground. She continued shrieking and shaking her finger at us.

Harriet, who was with us, thank goodness, answered her and then turned to us to explain when we asked, "What in the world is the matter with her?"

"Well" Harriet laughed, "She is terribly upset that you are so shockingly dressed and showing so much of yourselves. She is saying 'Porcarria,' which means pig."

There were a few Americans summering in Maccagno, sent to Italy to represent the companies they worked for in the states. What little social life we had revolved around them. It was interesting to see how other Americans engaged in the experience of spending a year or two in Italy.

There were the Lundbergs, Helen and Ralph, with their small baby. He worked for the U.S. embassy in Milan. Helen and Ralph were from near Boston with that 'down-eastern' accent that was so distinctive. Helen was blond with a rather matronly figure, about thirty. She was an excellent cook and every Saturday made Boston baked beans from scratch. The unusual thing about the Lundbergs was that they lived their life much as if they were still in the states. Instead of wanting to learn everything they could Italian, they spoke, cooked and dressed just as they had in Massachusetts. They even had their furniture made to order—their four-poster beds were just like the ones they had at home. To each his own, I suppose.

New Friends

Blossom and I heard music coming from the square each night and finally walked down to see what was going on. There were a few—maybe four or five—young men playing various instruments. They made pretty fair music. It was mostly polkas and waltzes. The square was right at the water's edge and from a little pub, strings of lights were hung across the square to buildings on the opposite side. In front of the pub were tables and chairs where the people had gathered. They all had heard of the Americans who had rented the villa, so when they saw us, they waved us over in a friendly fashion and asked us to sit down. We joined them and before long we found ourselves making new friends. We could not have guessed what pleasure we would have with some of these young people!

That first night as we danced with lots of the men, we realized this would be our chance to really learn Italian—none of these people spoke English! Each night we would go to the square, sit at a table and be joined by the same six or seven young men. They were unsophisticated country boys who found us odd—girls without chaperones who took the lead in conversations. How strange we must have seemed to them.

They willingly embarked on teaching us their language and through charades and laughter we would exchange ideas and differences in our cultures. We learned their names; Bruno, Luigi, Lodo, Ormando and Primo are all I can recall. Bruno was a rather large man, dark, with poor teeth, physically very strong, and seemed to be the leader of the group. Luigi had light brown hair, which was very long, almost to his shoulders. In 1938 the men and boys in the states wore their hair very short. Some even had crew cuts. The only people that Blossom and I had seen in the U.S. with longish hair were classical violin players and so before we ever knew any of their names, we nicknamed Luigi 'Violin.'

Lodo was the handsomest of the lot—strong jaw, short nose and nicely shaped haircut. He was the only one going to college and wore good looking shirts and trousers. He was quiet and sat on the sidelines as if he knew he wasn't really one of them, and yet he enjoyed our game of getting acquainted.

Their questions to us were intriguing. They wanted to know about our religion and asked specifically about the Catholics, which they were, and we weren't. However, having Catholic friends, we could tell some of their customs. When we said our friends went to confession regularly, they were amazed, and said they almost never did. They wanted to know what we ate and were fascinated with our breakfasts. They had never eaten bacon! We asked Harriet about bacon and she said the Italian word was panchetta fumicata (smoked pork) and that the Italians ate it rarely and then as an hors d'oeuvre.

They also had heard about maize (corn) that goes "pop-pop." "Oh yes, popcorn." Luigi spoke up and asked, "Could you send us some when you get home?" Of course, we could and would. We then explained in detail what they must do with it when it arrived. In our faulty Italian we told how to pop the corn. However, when we got home, we found that popcorn had come on the market already popped. "Much better," we thought so we bought a large bag and set it with large directions to not do anything to it but just eat it as it was. I am sorry to say we never heard from them. It could be some customs officer, seeing it was something unusual to eat, nabbed it.

We enjoyed the social life of the village through the months of July and August with our making new friends. These boys were regular folks and hanging out with them felt much more normal to us than the magical night life of the city. In the absence of Denis and Jeff we were able to relax be our old, sisterly selves, knitting and being aunts to our adorable nephews.

Hot Lips, Inc.

Not that we forgot about those two, of course. By this time, we had processed our photos and spent long hours remembering all the fun we had dancing, swimming, picnicking, and partying. One day Blossom and I were talking about the good time we had with Denis and Jeff over that last weekend together when they brought us to Maccagno. In the spirit of that fun weekend, we composed a letter to them calling attention to the Board of Directors of the Hot Lips and Co. I've kept this document and will quote from it, verbatim (as they say).

We decided to tap Blossom's experience as Mr. Morgenthaler's secretary at the furniture store and make it official and type-written:

Gentlemen:

Please be advised that at the last meeting of the skirt department of the board of directors of the HOT LIPS, INC. It was unanimously voted "that we had one swell time". It was also decided that the other members of the board were about the best dates on two continents. A discussion was held as to what was the most enjoyable event of the weekend. Because there were so many suggestions put before the meeting confusion ensued and no definite conclusion was reached. However, you might be interested to know that a few of the events heard above the din and confusion of the meeting were as follows:

1. The second installment of the thrilling serial "How to keep out of prison" or " Why girls leave home" as told by Just-a-minute Jephson and Pass-the-Beer Passadoro.

2. The testing of the fireworks and display.

3. Blossoms morning Gin Fizz.

4. The outstanding meetings of the Board of Directors.

5. The guzzling of beer at various times.

6. The beating of the drums by The Miss Becky Fahrig.

7. Crossing the borders. (Car never searched).

8. Rump steaks in general.

After the mail song was sung the question of the males was discussed and it was moved and seconded that a card should be sent to the headquarters of the home office at 119 Moffett Ave. Joplin, Mo. U.S.A.

The question of the next meeting was brought up and there were two definite wishes that it be soon. However, the time and place of the next meeting was left to circumstances owing to the absence of the rest of the BOARD.

The meeting closed with the passing of the motion to send a note of thanks to the chairmen of the entertainment committee.

Hoping to hear from you soon, we remain,

Very truly yours.

Becky & Blossom

Within a week this brought the desired effect: a telegram that read: "Board meeting tonight, Maccagno seven-thirty."

Denis and Jeff came often to Maccagno on Sundays when we would swim, hike and climb the mountains which were not very high and easy to climb. Harriet and Franco loved having them and the six of us spent many pleasant hours together. Franco came up every weekend and usually once during the week. One day when he came, he said he had a surprise for us.

"What is it? Tell us quickly!"

"It is a new apartment that I have found. Harriet, you must come and give it your O.K." The next morning, she went back with him, always on the train, and returned with much enthusiasm for the new home. We would be going back to Milan September 1st and dear Franco would have everything moved by then. The new address will be Via Vivaio 24. It is even closer to the center of town, which in Europe at that time was the most desired place to live.

The Boys' Party

Me & Boys

As summer wore on our friendship with the "boys" of Maccagno grew. We spent many hours in the day with them just "hanging out," to use the expression of today. When September grew near, the boys began talking about having a party for us. They wanted to have a dinner party for us, and we set a date. Neither Blossom nor I had the slightest idea what sort of 'party' it would be. We had always hung out at the square, our villa's garden, or at the edge of the lake where there was a small beach.

When the chosen night arrived, they called for us, all seven of them, and walked us to the home of Luigi. It was a very nice, modest home, typical for that region—stucco painted a light ochre and plastered walls inside painted white. No one else seemed to be home. We went right into the dining room where a large table was set for nine people. It had a white tablecloth with lace at the edge and some embroidery, and a small vase of flowers in the center. At Blossom's and my places were laid flowers called Stella d'Alpino (Star of the Alps) or 'Edelweiss' in German. This delicate blossom grows high in the mountains and is difficult to reach, so it is a great honor to have it given to you.

Luigi and Bruno served the food. It was quite apparent that Luigi's mother had cooked and arranged this event. Blossom and I were surprised and touched by the care and effort this unseen woman had taken. We wished she had been there so we could thank her and tell her how we had enjoyed the friendship of her son. She might have been upstairs, but she never appeared, which was a little surprising because, as I have said before, we were a curiosity among the town's people.

There were bottles of wine on the table, no water. The first course was antipasto, for which the Italians are famous. This appetizer is often quite elaborate with dozens of tasty tidbits arranged and beautifully garnished on a platter. Luigi brought it in with great flourish, a large tray filled with a wonderful assortment. As he held it aloft before lowering it for us to serve ourselves, we could feel a sort of excitement in each of them.

Then Luigi said in the voice of a master of ceremonies, "Signorine d'Amerrica, we have for you tonight a special treat."

All eyes were on us as they grinned and nodded their heads.

"It is pancheta fumicata!" Everyone clapped including Blossom and me.

Luigi lowered the tray for me to take some and I stopped dead. The pancheta fumicata had not been cooked—it was raw bacon.

I looked at Blossom and she at me. We recovered quickly for this was done with such caring we dared not spoil it. We served ourselves and ate the bacon, just a small amount, telling them that the other foods on the tray were so good we wanted to try everything.

Then they served us a steaming plate of pasta with red sauce. We were delighted with this meal and ate with gusto for it was late and we were hungry. They had not come to get us until nine o'clock and by now it was after ten. They cleared our plates away and we were totally unprepared for what followed. They brought in a complete dinner of roast beef, fried potatoes, green beans and tomatoes; this was followed by a salad course with hard rolls; then came a large variety of cheeses with bread, then fresh fruit and finally sweets and pastries with coffee. We were overwhelmed and over fed, but we certainly appreciated the effort that had gone into this party.

The boys were delighted that we enjoyed it so, for we could feel how important it was to them to be able to give something special to these Americans. They were fairly bursting with pride. At the end of the meal Bruno again filled all the wine glasses and stood to give a toast. Then, in his master of ceremonies voice, he called upon each one of us to say a few words. We were hard pressed to understand every word, but we certainly got the gist of what they were saying, and of course we too had to give a little speech. We struggled with our pigeon Italian, but our words were heartfelt and were met with cheers and clapping.

By now it was past midnight. All seven walked us home and said goodbye, we feeling like a pair of Snow Whites. These young men gave meaning to the Italian word "simpatico." In the many hours we talked and danced and learned from them we were aware that their lives had not always been easy. Four of them had fought in the campaign in Ethiopia just a few years before. We have often wondered how they fared the great conflict that was even at that moment bearing down on us. We prayed for their safety ...and do still.

Autumn

And so, the summer came and went. An easy, carefree time with Harriet and the little boys. Harriet had gone several times to the new apartment which met with her complete satisfaction. Franco had men from his factory move their belongings so that when we returned to Milan everything was there, albeit in much disarray.

Harriet had gone ahead of us. Linda, the boys, Blossom and I were to close the house in Maccagno and leave the next day. When we were finally ready to go to the train station, we found we had a lot to take and cope with. We had several suitcases, a large diaper bag, knitting bags, snacks for the children, and, of course, Frankie to carry.

All went well until we got to the station. Blossom bought the tickets and announced the train was about to leave. All of a sudden Linda, who had Frankie in her arms, put him down and hurried onto the train. Blossom, who handled the money was trying to get a porter and with no time to lose, I picked up Frankie in one arm, shifting my carry-ons to the other, Blossom grabbed the rest, and we all rushed to the train. The porter slid the suitcases on, I got on with Frankie and as Blossom hit the first step, she heard someone behind her yelling. Turning around, as the train began to move, she saw the porter skipping alongside asking for his tip. She still held the change from the tickets, so she just dumped it all into his out-stretched hand. The man ran alongside the moving train, counting his change, not about to give up his rightful lira. Soon he was running faster, holding out his hand for more. As Blossom yelled to me "I don't have enough money," I opened my purse and quickly gave her some bills which she threw to the breathless man. I'm sure it was the biggest tip he ever had.

When we got settled in our seats, we asked Linda, "What was that about? Why did you leave Frankie so and get on the train?"

"Oh, signorina, I am sorry. I saw a boy I had gone out with in Maccagno on my days off and I had never told him I was a domestic and I didn't want him to see me carrying a baby."

We could understand that.

City Life

Via Vivaio 24 was a modern stone building with huge outer doors that were locked every night. These doors were so mammoth that a smaller door was cut into one of them to permit entry to residents with a key who came home late at night. Instead of the cage-like elevator we had at Via Sidoli, this one was silent and enclosed, opening onto a hallway across from our front door. The new apartment was wonderfully spacious. Blossom and I had our own room though we still slept on the same two sofa-beds. There was a new couch in the large living room, a formal dining room and several balconies. It was exciting to be back in the city with such grand living quarters. There was much to be done and we pitched right in to help get settled.

Sometimes you don't realize what tension you feel until it is released. It is impossible to think of September 1938 in Europe without remembering the Munich Agreement. Hitler signed a pact with England and an agreement was also made between England and Italy. It seemed for a few days at least, that there would be no war.

It is testament to the optimism of youth, perhaps, that these events on the world stage held little interest for me at the time. I was far more concerned with the social life around me than these strange rumblings in foreign languages. When the agreement was signed and it seemed we had escaped war, I celebrated with those friends and family who understood the situation better than I. But it is only in retrospect that I can appreciate those perilous events. It was part of the enchantment of our trip that I could not grasp nor even be fully aware of the fearsome activities so near at hand.

Denis called and said he was going to Genoa for a few days. Franco announced he had tickets for a football game the next day. It was not football as we know it, but soccer. It was a chilly October day when Franco took Blossom and me to a huge stadium full of rabid fans. I was more interested in the people around us than I was in the game and I was fascinated with the food and drinks they had brought from home. In front of us were four men who produced a wide-mouthed gallon thermos jug. From a basket they passed out plates and forks and then served hot spaghetti from the thermos.

On the way out of the game we ran into Lodo, the handsomest of the boys from Maccagno. He asked if he could take me out the next evening. "Fine," I said and Franco gave him our new address. I really looked forward to it. However, when the time came, he never showed up. The fact that I was disappointed and hurt by his standing me up told me that my feelings for Denis were not as serious as I sometimes thought. I was young and infatuated, a romantic in love with romance. In fact, a week later we ran into Lodo again and once more made a date. Once more he stood me up. I was furious.

So much for dating Italian men. Basta! (Enough!)

Denis returned from Genoa and invited me to dinner at his apartment for a quiet evening to catch up. The euphoria after the Neville Chamberlain announcement had by this time completely evaporated and everyone was expecting the worst. Denis told me about the English people leaving Italy because of the war talk. Hitler strikes fear in everyone as he seems poised and determined to march his armies across Europe.

"Denis," I asked, "What will you do if war does come?"

He shook his head slowly and seemed for a moment in far-away thought before he roused himself and answered, "It depends. If Hitler attacks England, of course I must enlist. The future is so uncertain, Oh God, I wish it weren't so."

As he pulled me closer to him, I could feel his despair. As we sat there on his big leather couch my mind was racing. Why had I not been afraid? Wasn't I paying attention? Had I only been thinking of my world which was filled with such pleasure? I found politics boring—besides, all our news was in Italian, from the fascist government, and they didn't criticize Hitler.

I turned to Denis and asked, "Is it really bad?"

"God only knows what Hitler really is after."

It was our most subdued evening together.

On the way home I mentioned that Sunday was Harriet's birthday. "Lordy, she'll be thirty!" I said as only a twenty-one-year-old could.

Denis seemed to recover his spirits at this. "My dear girl! We must celebrate, Jeff and I will make arrangements."

Harriet's Birthday

Our celebration was settled for Saturday night the eighth of October. We decided to dress for the occasion. First, we went to Jeff's for cocktails, and then to Tantall's for a splendid dinner. As I looked across the table at Harriet whose large, widely set, blue eyes seemed to shimmer in the candlelight, I thought that thirty wasn't all that old, at least not for her.

After dinner we moved on to the Embassy Club where we could hear one of our favorite bands and dance. Everyone was in a festive mood and we all laughed more than usual. The orchestra struck up "Harvest Moon," an old favorite of ours from years of singing to the radio as we washed the dishes back home. Almost out of habit and our uninhibited mood, Blossom and I began to harmonize there at the table. Everyone stopped talking to listen, and the bandleader came over and asked us to sing with the band. Franco encouraged us — reminding us that we were 'Americanatas' and therefore could do anything we pleased. Denis and Jeff were delighted. We were such a far cry from any 'proper' dates they had ever had.

It was a thrill to move from the audience and walk across the dance floor to the little raised platform in front of the ten- or twelve-piece band. The band leader led us up to the single microphone on a sort of stand that could be moved wherever it was needed. Blah and I put our faces close together as we had seen in so many movies and started the song again.

> *"Shine on, shine on Harvest Moon, up in the Sky*
> *I ain't had no lovin' since January, February, June, or July*
> *Snow time ain't no time to stay outside and spoon,*
> *So, shine on, shine on Harvest Moon!"*

With Blossom's sweet high soprano and my alto, a third lower, our harmony sounded pretty good, if I do say so. It was such an exhilarating moment when, after the first couple of lines, suddenly the full sound of the orchestra filled in behind us. I could feel Blossom falter next to me—this was a strange experience for a normally shy person like her. I looked at her and saw a moment of terror in her eyes, but I took her hand and squeezed, and she recovered. My excitement and enjoyment seemed to buoy her spirit and together we really sang!

There was such an explosion of applause as we finished the song that I was afraid I would burst into tears. I looked around and everyone was on their feet! Jeff and Denis were hooting and even Harriet was shouting "Bravo!" The leader rushed up and took our hands and a torrent of Italian came out of his excited, happy face. Finally, it settled into, "Encore, encore! Per piachere sing another! Please, Signore!"

We looked at each other quizzically. What could we sing to follow that? Then Blossom shrugged and said, "Doodly-doo?" It was a campfire song and a favorite from childhood sleep-outs in the woods with our family back in Wisconsin.

The leader had a baffled look on his face. He turned to the band and asked them in Italian, "Who knows Doodly-doo?" Everyone shrugged. That's okay, I thought to myself, we never needed a band around the campfire...so, I said to the leader the word we learned in high school choir: "Acapella. We'll sing without accompaniment."

"Ah! Va bene!" And with a gesture, he gave us the stage...

. . . at least we began acapella, then the clarinet player caught the simple tune and soon the others joined in.

Oh, please play for me,
That sweet melody
Called doodly-doo, doodly-doo;
I like the rest,
But the part I like best,
Is doodly-doo, doodly-doo;

It's the simplest thing,
There isn't much to it,
You don't have to sing,
Just doodly-doo it!

I love it so,
Wherever I go,
It's doodly-doodly-doo!
Doodle-e-doodle-e-doo
Yeah!

And again, everyone in the place leaped to their feet and cheered. I looked at my sister who was blushing and trembling but laughing! Once more I took her hand and squeezed. My heart swelled almost to bursting, I was so thrilled and proud of us! We were far from trained singers, but we had both been in church and high school choirs, and, of course, we loved harmonizing to the radio in the living room.

We bowed and made out way back to the table where we hugged Harriet and wished her happy birthday! After that, whenever we went to the Embassy Club, we were asked to sing.

Our party was never less than enthusiastic in support and sweet Jeff nudged Denis and made a pitch for an RCA recording contract. Besides Harvest Moon, other favorites were, That Old Feeling, and Blue Moon. Doodly-Doo, was a favorite, with the audience eventually chiming in on the chorus.

Usually two songs were enough—we didn't want to push ourselves and it was just enough to make us feel like stars. That first night, we stayed until 1 a.m., then took Harriet and Franco home. The four of us went to Denis's for something to eat and to talk over the evening.

On the ninth, the actual day of Harriet's birthday, we played games with the children. In my diary I wrote, "Blossom acted funny and we all laughed until we cried."

She could turn her sweet, lovely face into all sorts of characters including our mother. By sucking in her cheeks and pursing her lips she transformed herself into "Miss Priss", a familiar member of the DAR (Daughters of the American Revolution). Mother was a prominent member in Joplin, and for several years when we were younger, Blah and I would dress up as George and Martha Washington for the annual convention. Since I was taller than Blossom, I had to be George.

Our good friend Ezio, the comical fellow we met on our stay in Padua, came by. He was such a gifted clown with his happy, expressive face. He and Franco acted up all evening and we all laughed again.

The social life was picking up for the fall season. In fact, it seemed to be more fun than ever—probably because Blossom and I were with Jeff and Denis so much.

The ladies' teas were abuzz with each new scandal—there seemed to be a fresh one every week. One concerned the smuggling of money out of the country. The value of the Italian lira was always unstable, so folks in northern Italy would frequently try to smuggle money into Switzerland. The government had restricted the amount of

Photo of them in costume ages eight and ten—
Blossom as George, Becky as Martha

money each person could take out of the country. But as the fears of war grew, so did thoughts of fleeing Italy. All the foreigners here were worried about losing their money. The value of the Italian lira was always unstable, so folks in the north would frequently try to smuggle money into Switzerland.

The latest ploy was to take a train to Lugano, in Switzerland, buy a ticket with a private compartment, roll down the window shades and put the large bills into the shade as you rolled it back up. The Italian customs officer would board the train and check the passengers for currency before the border was crossed. The crafty Italians would simply show their wallets and declare "niente!" Once safely across they could roll the shades down again and go to the bank.

October 13th was Blossom's birthday and Harriet asked Jeff and Denis for dinner. It was such a lively evening, even Linda was having fun watching us as she served the meal and brought in the cake with 24 candles on it. She had a cute little way of running her thumb along her cheek from ear to chin to indicate that she liked our beaus. She had heard Franco chanting to us when we first started to date Jeff and Denis saying, "Becky's got a beau-oh" and she imitated him with her thick accent "Beeckee sgot aboh!" This evening as she watched Blossom blow out the candles her eyes twinkled as she ran her thumb along her cheek.

The Kohners

Each week seemed to bring new experiences and one I shall never forget was our visit with the Kohners. They phoned and asked us to come for the evening. We had our usual dinner at eight o'clock and at nine walked a short distance to the bus and rode across town to their apartment. The Kohners were Russian, and on the way to their apartment Harriet filled us in on some of their history. They were what was known as White Russians. Before the revolution toward the end of the first world war, they had been successful manufacturers of samovars, owning a large factory and beautiful home. When the communists took over, they sent the Kohners to Siberia, took over the factory and moved into their house. I think Mr. Kohner died in Siberia and the family emigrated to Europe. Evidently, they were always on the move, trying out different countries. They were now back in Milan after a period in Austria. We were greeted with great affection and warmth, for they had not seen Harriet and Franco for a long time.

The family consisted of Mrs. Kohner, her daughter Lucy, Lucy's husband Sergio Gambarov and Sergio's mother. A son Gary was not there. Mrs. Kohner was a grandmotherly type, a strong full face, crinkles around grey eyes that were kind and piercing at the same time. Her daughter Lucy was a beautiful woman in her late thirties. Her hair was full and luxurious, framing her face with soft curls, and her skin was smooth and fair. Sergio and his mother were Persian, with dark complexion and dark hair. He was very tall and rather portly which made him appear huge. Franco commented about his size and his mother said when he was born, he weighed thirteen pounds.

There was much talking and exchanging of pleasantries, all in Italian of course, which gave Blossom and me time to look around at the interesting room into which we had been ushered. It was a large dining room and had a great 'lived-in' look about it. There were comfortable chairs, books, newspapers and a radio on a small bookcase. In the center of the room was a round dining table covered with a linen cloth and laden with food. The one thing I remember about the food was the great mound of black Caviar.

Franco sidled up to me and whispered, "Be sure and eat some of the caviar. It is Sergio's business for he is an importer." And to Sergio he said, "How is business, Sergio? Are you selling a lot of caviar?"

With a nod Sergio replied "Very good. Everyone is living the good life before it is too late." He spoke good English but with a thick accent. He leaned over the table and spread a piece of dark bread with the glistening, beaded delicacy—slathering it on as we might do with peanut butter. He handed a slice of it to Blossom and another to me.

"You do not know caviar, no?" he said. "Well, this is a good time to learn for this is the best from Iran. The sturgeon of the Caspian Sea produce the finest in the world. We have a source among the fishermen in the village of Chalus."

I tasted and found it salty but delicious. While we had been introduced to caviar earlier at one of Doro Ausenda's 'teas', it was from Sergio that I gained my first real appreciation of this delicacy.

Everyone was given a drink, from vodka to coffee and we settled around the table to enjoy their hospitality. Franco noticed that Mrs. Kohner was drinking not vodka but a powerful liqueur with the delicate message on the label, which Sergio translated for us: "From the little flowers grown on the steppes of Russia." I cannot recall the name of this drink with this innocent slogan, but when I tasted it, I found it had a kick like a mule.

"How is it Signora that you don't drink vodka?" Franco asked.

She shot back, "If you had been as cold as we were you would drink this, too."

She raised her glass. Eyes smiling and relief in her voice, she proposed a toast, "To the warmth of the Italian sun and the warmth of our good friends here."

We all raised our glasses, and Franco, ever the diplomat, said, "And to our good friends visiting here."

It was very apparent that Sergio was a brain. He spoke eight languages and knew the world well. His mother said that by the age of two he was speaking Russian and Farsi, the language of Persia. When the conversation got too involved, Lucy asked Blossom and me if we played bridge. Yes, we did. A table was set up and Sergio joined us for bridge. He was such an expert that a couple of times after we played a hand, he would put the cards back, remembering exactly which cards each person held and reviewed the hand showing us a better way to play it.

The most memorable part of the evening came when we gathered in a close circle while they spoke of their trials and ordeals in Russia. Mrs. Kohner told of the cold in Siberia. They were sent there for a number of years and she said their legs were changed by the cold. She described it as something like the pain of shin splints—getting deep in the bone. She said it also affected their skin and that they would never get over it.

When they were finally released there was nothing left for them in Russia and they were considered the enemy. They had friends in Italy and had come to Milan with a short visa allowing them to stay one year. The year was nearing its end and they talked of where they could go to start a new life. They spoke of Australia and as they talked, I remembered Harriet's comment to us shortly after we arrived, when she said, "Guard your passport, it is probably the most precious thing you have."

Blossom asked if they had thought of the United States but there was some technical reason they could not come here. It moved me so, to sit and hear their anxiety over the future. How many others in Europe at that moment were doing the same thing? It was one o'clock in the morning before we said goodbye and took our leave of these charming, gifted people.

Years later I asked Harriet where they settled. She told me they were able to go to Germany and find a decent life. Their son Gary, whom we did not meet and who was blond and as handsome as a movie star, was drafted into the German army and killed in the war.

We took the elevator down and started walking to the bus stop some four blocks away. Blossom and I walked ahead along the deserted street. It was wide and lined with trees which made shadows from the streetlights. We were some distance ahead of Harriet and Franco who were sauntering slowly when we heard someone holler. It seemed to come from across the street and ahead of us. Then it came again, two voices this time, women's voices with an angry tone. And in a minute, we could see them screaming as they came toward us on the other side of the street. Of course, Blossom and I had no idea what they were saying but they seemed to be directing it at us. The next moment, to our great surprise, we heard Franco answering them in a loud voice. Whatever he said shut them up. We had stopped and by this time Harriet and Franco had caught up with us.

Harriet was laughing and Franco with a chuckle said, "Do you know what they were saying?"

"No, what was the matter with them?"

"They were telling you to get off the street; this is their territory. They thought you were prostitutes. "

Remembering the berating we had been given by the old woman in Maccagno, it seemed that we were destined to be yelled at by Italian women of every class and condition. We laughed all the way to the bus stop.

Blossom kept saying, "If that doesn't beat all."

Turning Homeward

The end of October brought me a letter that disturbed me greatly. It was from Jim Castner whom we last saw standing on the pier waving goodbye, in New York. Early in the year he had written in answer to our letters thanking him for the lovely send off, the suitcase and the marvelous dinner at the Rainbow Room in New York. In that letter he had said he too had enjoyed the evening and hoped to see us when we returned. Now came this letter addressed to me and I was shocked when I read it. I can't remember his exact words but it went something like this.

> *Dear Becky,*
>
> *I have thought about you a lot this year, in fact I can't forget you. I feel there is something between us, something that was there in New York. How else do we explain the silence between us when we were alone, and Blossom was dressing. I would like to come over to Italy and accompany you home. We could get better acquainted and find out what it is between us.*
>
> *Hoping to hear from you,*
> *Love,*
> *Jim*

I put the letter down with a sick heart. That dear, sweet man wanting to come all the way over here to go home with us. How could I tell him I felt nothing special for him? The silence he spoke of was awkward and embarrassing as I recalled. I had always felt it more difficult to handle a situation where I cared less for someone than they did for me. Even as a child I hated the thought of hurting someone's feelings. Now I was faced with this dreadful task of answering him. I did write a letter asking that we just remain friends and saying that both Blossom and I would enjoy seeing him again. But of course, we never did.

Autumn was slipping by and it was time to think of booking our passage home. The day we went downtown to make these arrangements we stopped by our favorite tiny hat shop to order new hats. By this time the milliner had come to know and grow a bit fond of us, I think. At least she would now allow us to actually try on the hats we were interested in. Still, one didn't buy the actual hat in the shop for that was just a sample. Some of the styles that year were frightful, but hats were a must, and we tried on many before we found what we liked. Mine was a navy blue felt with a turned-up brim all the way around. Blossom's was black with a feather.

Buying luxuries like a couple of hats makes me aware that a word about money seems necessary here. How could two daughters of a middle-class mid-western family have possibly afforded to spend a year in Europe? We must admit that we were world-class moochers this entire time. Certainly, Harriet and Franco had sponsored us for our daily needs of food and shelter even allowing for the monthly $100 bill from our parents. And all the nightclubs and restaurant tabs were graciously picked up by Jeff and Denis who never complained. In fact, given the social norms of the time, I believe they would have been downright offended if we had tried to wrestle the check away from them. So, we went home with clear consciences that we had played our parts perfectly well. 'Moochers' is only my retrospective self-judgment.

The social life continued, and Denis and I did something together on an average of four times a week. Our good times with Jeff and Blossom were usually board meetings of Hot Lips and Co. We went to the theater, the opera, the movies which were dubbed in Italian if they were American films. It was there that we saw the wonderful new Disney movie "Snow White". Snow White's singing voice was dubbed by an Italian opera singer. In fact all the dialog was dubbed into Italian and there were English subtitles for the sake of us Americans.

We loved these evenings, but most of all we loved going to the Embassy Club and dancing. Jeff and Denis wanted to learn "American" dancing. It was faster than they danced—sort of a mild jitterbug that just delighted them. As Denis and I whirled around the polished floor to the blare of the band I heard him exult, "I can't believe I'm doing this."

As our time drew short, we treasured the family. The little boys were adorable, and we loved playing with them. We knitted each of them a little suit for Christmas. By the time Christmas came we found ourselves with mixed emotions. How could we leave? And yet the yearning for home seemed to grow stronger the nearer we came to January.

Christmas was like Christmas everywhere, filled with giving, singing, trees and, in our Joplin home, Santa Claus. The Italians have the children's surprise on Twelfth Night representing the time the wise men got to Bethlehem. There were many gatherings of friends and loved ones. By the time New Year's Eve arrived, we found our minds turning towards home.

Dickie and Frankie

Leave Taking

All year we had been gathering things that we wanted to take home. Now it was January and we began to organize them and put them into the big empty suitcase Jim had given us. One of the last things we would purchase to take with us would be cheese. My dad's favorite was Gorgonzola, one of Italy's best products, and what better gift to take to him than that. The day we did most of our packing, little Dickie was eager to help. We had our bags lined up in the hall giving us more space to organize. When we would return from the bedroom with an armload to pack, we would find that Dickie had placed in a suitcase a hammer or a screwdriver or some other tool from his father's toolbox. He was just trying to be like us, and we tried to take the things out so he would not see us, letting him think he had helped us pack. When we got home and unpacked, we found that he had the last word, for there, in the bottom of one of the bags, was a screwdriver.

Neither Blossom's nor my hands had been idle these past months. We had knitted, sewed, embroidered, and made many lovely garments to wear or pretty things to have—such as our shadow-stitch embroidered handkerchief holders. Without the old steamer trunk, which was quickly disintegrating, it was going to be a squeeze. So, we bought some beautiful raffia baskets which served us well.

We were terribly excited to think of going home. Harriet and Franco had a magnificent party for us. All our friends came to say goodbye. Everyone dressed in stunning formal clothes, looking so elegant (Jeff and Denis wore tails) and giving us one of the sweetest memories of the year.

We were to sail from Trieste on Tuesday, January 17th but there were some things we had to do one last time. Saturday, the 14th Denis and I went out for dinner to the little place in the country that we had gone to many times before. We talked cheerfully and pretended it was not the last time we would be alone like this. I had asked Denis for a photo of himself and he gave me one from a ski trip in the Alps last year. I wished I could have been with him there!

By now it was clear that Chamberlain's "peace in our time" was a naïve miscalculation. Hitler went right on preparing for war.

"Is it really going to happen?" I asked. "I just don't want to believe that something as dreadful as war could destroy the peace of this beautiful continent and these wonderful people."

Gazing at his handsome face, I could see the muscles tighten in his cheek. He drove on a bit before answering,

"I'm afraid so," he said, glancing at me with a quick intensity. I felt a chill as I saw that he knew war was inevitable. He took my hand, his voice softened, "and it's good you are going home. That's where you should be now."

When we drove up in front of the apartment, he parked and turned toward me. We looked at each other for a long time, eyes locked before he spoke. "I must tell you; I think you are a remarkable person, and I've loved the time we've spent together. I saw a line of poetry recently, Ezra Pound, I believe. He wrote: 'Whatever comes, we shared an hour that was sunlit, and the most high gods could make no better boast, than to have watched that hour as it passed.'"

We kissed deeply and I told him how I cherished the time we spent together, and I thanked him for loving me so sweetly. Then quickly he got out and came around for me. He unlocked the building and let me in, as we stood in the 'doorway within the door' he gave me a kiss just as if we would be seeing each other next week, handed me the key and shut the door.

Sunday was busy spending as much time with the little boys as possible. In the evening the six of us went to Giannino's for a last dinner together. Jeff and Denis liked Harriet and Franco so much and vice versa. It was an evening filled with laughter and fun, lots of toasts to each other and everyone signed a menu for both Blossom and me to have as a wonderful reminder of the evening and yes, all the other exceptional meals we had in that outstanding restaurant.

Saying goodbye to the little boys was so difficult and we just had to hope that they would remember us. It was Monday morning and Harriet and Franco were going with us on the train to Trieste. It was a major effort getting all our impedimenta including an overnight bag for Harriet and Franco, to the station. Linda and the little boys came down to the street door to see us off. As we said goodbye to Linda and hugged her, we were aware how much she had given to us that year. We had honed our Italian on her, laughed and kidded around, learned some things from her and wished we had such a person to help at home. Most importantly, because Linda had been there to take the reins, she had freed Harriet to travel with us and be our guide through so much of Italy on this trip.

Franco was a jewel, taking care of everything when we got to the station. A few minutes before we got on board, Denis and Jeff appeared. They had flowers for us and made jokes about life never being the same in Milan. My last embrace with Denis found my heart pounding as I whispered, "I'm leaving part of my heart here."

He answered, "And you are taking my heart with you."

We stepped on the train as it started to move and, in a minute, he was gone.

Denis on Skis

Trieste

Arriving, we checked into a hotel then went to the port to see about the luggage we had sent directly to the ship. All was well. The Saturnia was docked looking very grand indeed, like her sister ship, the Vulcania.

Having time before dinner, Harriet and Franco walked us around showing us Trieste. It sits at the top end of the Adriatic Sea and over the centuries has been claimed by several countries. One of the features Trieste is known for is "The Bora," a terrific wind that blows down from the Alps at certain times of the year. Consequently, many items around the city were tied down or lashed with ropes to metal loops in the concrete sidewalks or walls. They had a network of ropes strung around the sidewalks of Trieste for the pedestrians to hang on to. There were stories of cars and trucks being blown off the roads.

Sleep that night was fitful. The dread of saying goodbye and the excitement of sailing the next day filled my mind, making me toss and turn. We were to sail at noon which gave us a leisurely morning. Harriet and Franco accompanied us on board and helped us find our stateroom. Again, as in leaving New York, friends were dear in sending us Bon Voyage letters and telegrams. One from Denis read, "All is grey and gloom here since it must be so. Thank you for the memories and fare thee well."

The most difficult time, of course, was saying goodbye to Harriet and Franco. By the time they walked back down the gangplank, leaving us at the rail, and the ship began to move we were all in tears. We waved until we could see them no longer, then hearing the call that lunch was being served Blossom grabbed my arm and said, "Let's go, I'm starved"

How glad I was to have her with me. Her enthusiasm, as always, carried me along as we went down the stairs and entered into the life of the voyage, one that would carry us home.

The Voyage Home

I t was easy for us to feel at home for this was the sister ship to the Vulcania, almost its twin in design and layout. Nor did it take long to get acquainted with some of our fellow passengers. We were learning that there is an attraction between people in a crowd of this sort—natural friends seem to gravitate toward each other. By the second day we found ourselves gathered around a table in the lounge, getting to know one another better and making future plans.

There was Dr. Massue Monat from Montreal, a dentist whom we called simply "Doc". He was short, quick, with a flair for having a good time. Another doctor was Harold O'Connell from New York. Blond, tall, a friendly manner, extremely nice, and eager to be a part of our group. Then we had a prince from Russia, Nicolai Obolensky, the brother of Serge Obolensky who at that time was a well-known designer. We all called him "Prince" and thoroughly enjoyed him. He was medium build, dark hair, lean face with a very kind and caring expression. His manner was polite and somewhat serious—well spoken with a subtle accent.

Charles Sonnenfeld was a young man in his twenties traveling with his parents, whom he forsook to be with us. He had an accent as well, and a great deal of charm. Frank Harding a was tall, young, handsome American and asked us to call him Buck. The last of the males in our gang was Charles Wheeler, a young, blond, good looking boy from California. The females other than Blossom and me were Elizabeth Ewing Bahonyi a New York girl in her twenties with long stringy hair and a formal manner. There was also a girl with a strange name that I can't remember. She was an interpretive dancer and quite foreign. Most of these new friends were traveling alone and it was only natural that we would band together to enjoy the trip.

This sailing was also a cruise with the first stop at Dubrovnik, Yugoslavia. We were there only half a day but made the most of it.

We rented cars without the driver and we were in the one driven by Charles Wheeler. It was a huge touring car without a top and, since the day was sunny and mild for January, we had a ball. The ever-present street market gave us an opportunity to buy trinkets and funny little embroidered hats.

Back on board we dove right into the life of a holiday at sea. The next day we were in Patras, Greece and I must say I was disappointed. Greece to me had always held visions of beautiful Greek ruins but Patras had none of that. Again, we were there only a short time and glad to get back on the ship where the fun was.

We sailed around the toe of Italy and stopped again at Naples. This time we had a very short time there arriving in the late afternoon and leaving at midnight. On the morning of the 21st we arrived at Palermo. It was fascinating. We hired a guide for we had a full day there with perfect weather so we wanted to make the most of it. Palermo was filled with color—the native dress, the buildings and dozens of little carts painted over every inch with bright decorations. The guide took us into an elaborate church with a huge crypt. Upon entering it we were astounded to see hundreds of skeletons and shelves with rows and rows of human bones all arranged in order; the skulls all lined up together, the arms, hips and so forth. All these were the remains of monks from centuries past whose order somehow connected to this church.

We had two days at sea before reaching Gibraltar and life on board ship took on a charm of its own. The days were sunny and pleasant. Our little gang spent afternoons on deck. The sea was calm and at three o'clock bullion was served from carts together with crisp celery, huge green olives and French bread.

Blossom and I had time to talk about our feelings. We were both looking forward to going home. One's own country has a great appeal when you are away from it for any length of time. We were not particularly homesick but gave voice to a few desires.

"I will love having a good old hamburger again" Blossom mused. And I answered, "I am dying for a Mars bar."

And then I asked, "Will you miss Jeff?"

"No, but then we were never in love like you and Denis. But you seem to be getting along pretty well without him."

"I know, I loved it all. But I'm not sad. It was sort of like dating a movie star and living on a cloud but knowing all the time that this was not my real life. For some reason I think he feels the same way."

And then Blossom said in a quiet way, "I'll say you're not sad. You're enjoying the men on this trip too much to be sad."

"Well," I responded, "How often do you find a real, live prince to flirt with?"

"Oh, jees! You're right."

On the 22nd of January we were in Gibraltar and since we had done a lot of sight-seeing inside the rock when we were there before, this time we looked in the shops and did some shopping. Perfume was the thing to get we were told. No tax or duty so the price was right. It seemed to be a specialty there as many shops sold nothing but perfume. But it was not as easy to choose as I had imagined. When I said I wanted some perfume the man brought out a little tray about eight inches square marked off with tiny cubby holes with a little-bitty vial in each hole. There were hundreds of them. He wanted to know which I wanted to smell. I told him something spicy and Blossom wanted more flower essence. Well, it took a while but we finally did buy some for ourselves and for mother.

It only now occurs to me that within a short nine months the Saturnia would be considered an enemy ship by the British forces at Gibraltar. There were rumors flying that submarines were watching the straits, but we had no idea whose. Probably both sides. Everyone could remember the submarine war that the Germans waged in 1914-18. The passenger liner Lusitania had been sunk by a torpedo from a U-boat. Over a thousand drowned!

Back on the ship we sailed safely out through the straits and into the Atlantic Ocean on our way to Lisbon. The fun we had in Lisbon was mostly our gang seeing the city together. By now the weather was getting colder and we stayed inside once back on the ship.

Our last stop was the Azores which did not leave a lasting impression on me. But as we left, we were very aware of the ocean stretching before us. Once, when we were two or three days out, I was walking the deck for exercise I stopped at the rail and looked at the vast expanse of water. The sea was choppy, and we chugged through the waves seemingly making little progress. I realized how small we were, and my thoughts went back to Columbus and how he must have felt in his small ship with no engine, not knowing where he would end up. I turned and walked toward the lounge with the warm lights and friends laughing and counted my blessings.

Return to New York

As we neared the end of our voyage together, we all sat around and talked about what we would each be doing when we landed. Blossom and I were going back to the Hotel Taft for a night or two. During this past year, our brother Dick and his wife Gladys had moved to New Jersey where he had a good job with du Pont, of course. This meant our dear parents were at home alone for the first time in over thirty years. I imagined them on the porch of the house at 718 North Byers waiting for us.

Dick, like the good son that he is, and the only son, and followed Daddy's lead and more, getting a degree in chemical engineering from the University of Michigan. He then landed a job at du Pont and in 1939 he was living with his wife, Gladys and new baby Carol in Pompton Lakes, New Jersey. We planned to spend a few days with them before heading on to Joplin.

When he could, Dick would come to New York and pick us up. We knew he was not able to get there to meet the boat. This was okay with us as we rather liked the idea of a day or two in the big city. We liked it even more when we found out Frank Harding, Charles Wheeler and Elisabeth Bahonyi would also be in the city for a day or two. We decided to meet and have a drink together at some snazzy place. Of course, we chose the Waldorf Astoria. Harold O'Connell who lived in New York City heard us talking and wanted to join us. Oh, it would be such fun to have our gang gather at that lovely hotel.

We were to dock at noon on Monday the 6th of February, 1939. We were up early you can bet, having a last luxury breakfast and then getting our packing done so we could be on deck to witness our entrance into that famous harbor. It was a grey day, but nothing could dampen our spirits. The most beautiful sight imaginable is the Statue of Liberty from the deck of a returning ship. It made lumps in our throats. How it must impress and gladden the hearts of the immigrants who pour through this harbor. To glide past this lovely statue and see Manhattan Island with its thrilling skyline gave me a feeling of such love and gratitude for my country—I cherish that memory and those feelings still.

After checking in at the Taft Hotel we had a light lunch and then went out to enjoy the city. As Blossom and I walked along amid the crowds taking it all in, we noticed how wonderful everything looked. Especially the people. We began to take a good look at individuals as they passed us. How beautifully dressed they were. Everyone, but everyone, was well groomed and had a certain style that made us comment, "This is the best looking public in the world."

Our get-together at the Waldorf at five o'clock was as delightful as we had hoped. We tried to act as if it were an everyday occurrence but inside, we were a little awed. No one but Doc O'Connell had been there before, so we all talked about how it felt. When we parted of course we all hoped we would meet again someday. And indeed, one day I would be in Montreal and be the guest of Doc Monat; Blossom would have a date with Doc O'Connell the next September while visiting our brother in New Jersey.

Dick picked us up on Wednesday and we spent four lovely days with him and Gladys. We had sent some of the luggage on home and kept a few bags that we would need with us. In one of these bags were some gifts for relatives. When we got to Dick's he placed them in the bedroom for us and we didn't pay much attention where they were. About the end of the third day we began to smell something pretty strong. We traced it to the suitcase that was very near a heat register. When we opened it we found the Gorganzola cheese warm and ripe and everything in the bag including the suitcase itself reeking of cheese.

Dick made us feel better saying, "If that's the worst trouble you have with all you are handling you are lucky."

He saw to our train tickets and reminded us that we were to stop overnight at the Evanses in Wilmington on the way home. The Evanses were glad to see us and hear about our trip and we loved being there. Early the morning of the 16th we boarded the train for the last leg. We had been spoiled with Dick and Mr. Evans getting our reservations and checking our luggage, so we never had to give it a thought. We didn't even have to notify Mother and Dad when to meet us for, true to his word, Mr. Evans sent them a telegram that read: "Girls will arrive at 9:10 the evening of 17th. They look fine and have had a great experience."

The Last Lap

We were on the last lap and to our surprise, we both felt tired. It was nice to just sit back and let the scenery roll by. Of course, we chatted but for the most part we relaxed. Lunch in the dining car was uneventful. There were few people on the train. The afternoon was slipping by as Blossom and I sat facing each other reading. Just then the conductor came in and stood by us. He had taken our tickets in the morning and now he appeared a little hesitant as he held our tickets in his hand and said;

"Young Ladies, we have a little problem."

A bit alarmed Blossom said, "Oh jees, now what."

"Well, you have a coach ticket and yet you have paid for a Pullman reservation."

"Oh, are we in the wrong place?"

"No, that is not the trouble. You see in order to sleep in the Pullman car you have to have a first-class ticket. You have the choice of either paying a little more to get a first-class seat and sleep or you could sit up here in the coach and we will refund you the money you paid for the Pullman."

Well, Blossom and I looked at each other. The money back sounded good but did we want to sit up all night? Blossom spoke up and asked, "Do we have to decide now?"

"No, you think about it and I'll be back after a while."

As he walked away my eyes followed him down the aisle, the blue uniform gracefully moving toward the door. For a moment I sat staring, not focusing on anything until, with some embarrassment, I realized I was staring directly at a man facing me. He was near the end of the car, some eight rows ahead of us and across the aisle. He was looking right at me and beckoning with his finger for me to come. He was a fine-looking older gentleman with grey hair, not unlike my own father.

Without giving it a second thought, I walked up and sat down on the seat facing him.

"Yes sir?"

He leaned forward and in a tender voice asked, "Do you need any money?"

Surprised, I warmed to him immediately,

"Oh, no sir, we have money. We are just debating whether to spend it."

"Fine" he replied, "then will you do me the honor of being my guests for dinner this evening?"

I laughed with delight, turned, and motioned to Blossom who was staring at us with a perplexed expression. As she sat down, I explained the situation and we introduced ourselves to this kind man. His name was Foster, and he traveled a great deal for business. He was most interesting and also interested, which made for wonderful conversation. We sat together and visited until the porter came through announcing dinner.

The table was set with the usual crisp white linen cloth, sparkling glassware and fresh flowers. Since becoming a traveler by rail, I recognized this sense of well-being when seated in a dining car. Mr. Foster sat across from us and after our cocktails arrived carefully put his large damask napkin in his lap, leaned back with great satisfaction, took a sip and said, "This is a pleasure indeed for me to have such lovely young company. The last time I had a guest for dinner on the train she was a DAR, and you know the type."

It was all Blossom and I could do to keep from laughing for, yes, we knew the type. Immediately we both remembered Harriet's birthday in Milan and the fun we had with "Miss Priss" at our dear mother's expense.

We had helped her on many occasions for the DAR. When we were small, she had dressed us as George and Martha Washington to be greeters at a reception for the DAR; and when I was seventeen, I had served as a page at their state convention in Kansas City. But we didn't let on about mother to Mr. Foster. We saw him the next morning at breakfast and soon after that he got off at St. Louis. Oh, yes, we did pay for the Pullman and had a good night's sleep.

The last stage home was the longest of any leg of the trip, for we were getting anxious to get home and see Mother and Dad. The train was on time, and so at 10 after 9 we stepped off and into the arms of our loving parents.

After hugs and kisses and a few tears daddy said, "Welcome home, my honeys. You have been gone a year, a month, a week and a day."

The End

Afterword

Now, sixty years later I can tell you how many of those lives turned out.

Hill (Jeff) Jephson married after the war and stayed in Milan until his retirement to Scotland. He stayed close friends with Harriet and Franco.

Harriet and Franco had another child, Guido, in 1945, and lived a long happy life together until Franco's death in 1996. Harriet lived in Italy until her death at 92 in August 2000.

Dickie married, had three little girls and divorced. He is now a grandfather living in Bergamo Italy.

Frankie died when he was 15 from the illness that had plagued him all his life.

Blossom married after the war to Frank Cole Jr. of Providence, Rhode Island. They had two sons: Francis Sessions, and Harry. They enjoyed 52 years of happy married life until Frank died in 1998.

And I corresponded with Denis that summer of 1939 and was not surprised to realize that I did not long for him. If the happy times with him in Italy felt like a dream then, they seemed more so when I was home. Almost unreal. His letters spoke of the threat of war and his desire to become a pilot in the Royal Air Force, which he did. War broke out between Germany and England that September. I learned later that he fought with the RAF in the victorious Battle of Britain. Then he was transferred to the desert war in Egypt in 1943 where he was killed in a plane crash. I am sure that he never forgot nor did I, the laughing, happy, sunny days in Italy.

At the same time that war began in Europe my life changed dramatically. On Sept 7th I met Stuart Landrum on a blind date. It was almost instant love for both of us. He was handsome, strong and made me feel warm and content, happy to be here and know that I would live in the

United States. I wrote to Denis and told him. He answered just before he left for his basic training, congratulating Stu and giving me best wishes. I did not hear from him again but Harriet told me he married and had a couple of happy years with his wife.

Stu and I were married January 28, 1940. We had 57 happy and eventful years together, and never once did I doubt that I had married my true love. We had three children, Michael, Stuart Jr. and Rebecca. Stu died Sept 16, 1997.

Postscript

Rebecca Ann, 'Becky' Fahrig returned to her family in Joplin, Missouri on February 27, 1939. Six months later, on September 1, Germany invaded Poland and World War Two began, erasing the Europe she had just visited from all but her memory. Harriet and Franco's family suffered many hardships during the war. During the intensive bombing of Milan, Franco moved his family to the town of Varese in the foothills of the Alps.

Becky was 21 when she and Blossom returned from Europe. The trip surely must have felt to them like a Hollywood fantasy. Hobnobbing with the expatriate society of Milan, consisting of two or three hundred wealthy, influential British and American businesspeople, and Italian spouses who gathered in their spacious apartments and often in the many restaurants and nightclubs of that city. The sisters had many happy experiences, which, like the bubbles in a flute of fine champagne, would quickly vanish. The nightclub bands would fade away, never to be seen again following the havoc and destruction of World War II.

The America they returned to was still suffering through the Depression. Their home was still an unremarkable middle-class dwelling at 119 Moffet Avenue in Joplin, Missouri. Their father still went to work maintaining the idle DuPont dynamite plant. There were no Alpha Romeo's on the gravel roads of the American Midwest.

In early September 1939, the phone rang in the Fahrig home and Becky's mother, Florence answered, listened, and called, "Beck!"

Handing the instrument to her daughter, she whispered with a note of judgment in her voice, "It's that Rod St. Clair!"

"Hello?" There was a little thrill in Becky's voice. She had dated Rod briefly before the trip to Italy, and she liked him. Rod was a big young man (6'2") with a large extrovert's personality.

"Hey, Sugar-toes, there's somebody I want you to meet!" Rod made it sound as if she had just won the lottery.

"Oh, really?" Becky caught his mood.

"Yeah! He's a Jayhawk and a Phi-Psi brother, and a ton of fun!" (Both men were recent grads from Kansas U, and members of Phi Kappa Psi fraternity).

So, Becky agreed to a double date with Rod and his girlfriend, Jane Lawrence, for the following Saturday night. That's how she met Stu Landrum. She was relieved to discover that Stu was much different than Rod, who could be a bit overwhelming. Stu was a quiet, bespectacled young man in his mid-twenties, five foot nine, several inches shorter than Rod, and just right for dancing with Becky who was five-six. Also, there was a strong resemblance to Denis Passadoro in stature and countenance with one important difference – Stu was an American. Becky might have thought, "Here's that American Denis I'm looking for!"

Rod and Stu were partners in a small Conoco gas station in northern Oklahoma, not far from their hometown of Baxter Springs, Kansas. In the back seat of Rod's car on that first date, while they were laughing at one of Rod's jokes, Becky noticed that Stu had perfect, beautiful teeth. On such trifles do our lives pivot. Becky and Stu went out on dates together several times that month of September 1939. Stu would work at the Conoco Station, clean up at his parents' house in Baxter Springs, then drive the eighteen miles to Joplin. So, it was dark by the time he picked Becky up

Stuart M Landrum

for their date. Perhaps overcoming these obstacles provided a spur to their relationship.

One of the movies they saw together that September of '39 was *The Wizard of Oz*. When Judy Garland as Dorothy declared at the end, "There's no place like home!" Becky found tears streaming and took comfort on Stu's shoulder with his clean handkerchief. They dated for only a few weeks that autumn during which love bloomed and the mighty matrimonial question was asked and answered affirmatively. Meanwhile, life was throwing more obstacles into the couple's path.

Stu received a new offer to leave the gas station for another job with Conoco: traveling and selling merchandise to the Conoco gas stations in the southwest states - starting immediately. For the next three months Stu was on the road in Texas, New Mexico, and Arizona. The relationship he'd begun with Becky was now restricted to the written expression of nearly 90 letters that passed between them. At one point rather late in the courtship she realized that she had not yet seen him in daylight!

But if Becky thought she'd found an American equivalent to the wealthy, sophisticated, British, Denis Passadoro, she had a lot to learn. And it might take more than daylight to learn all there was to know. . .

Stuart Milton Landrum was the elder son of Wesley Talmadge Landrum and Elizabeth 'Bertha' Haskins Landrum, a young couple who began their family just as another great opportunity arose in their lives – the First World War, which increased the demand for lead and zinc. Wesley was working as a miner in the Carthage Missouri area when three wealthy men decided he had the management skills to supervise a new mine for them.

The new mine was successful. Soon Wes Landrum was the boss of three mining operations in Picher, Oklahoma, just south of the Kansas state line. Since it was a new area, the "Town" of Picher was only a raw mining camp in a muddy field, and the first home for Wes, Bertha and two-year-old Stuart was a tar-paper shack. With time and success, the family's living quarters improved but still below modern expectations. In Picher, Wes had improved the property by adding a large garden and even raising pigs, chickens, and a milk cow. I remember Bertha, my grandmother, telling me once, "There's no tyranny like a cow." By the mid 1920's, Wes's mines were paying off handsomely. He was finally able to build a large Victorian house on Main Street in Baxter Springs and Bertha had indoor plumbing at last. Bertha, the daughter of a farmer named George Haskins in central Kansas, was no stranger to such hardships.

Bertha Haskins Landrum

Wesley T. Landrum

A skinny little kid running wild through the miners' camp, playing with the mules and donkeys, roughhousing with the other kids, Stuart grew up thinking there was no better career than mining engineer. He wanted to follow in his father's footsteps. His father had a different idea. Wes forbad young Stuey to become a miner because he knew the risks. There was a family legend about Wes inspecting an empty mine with another man. Suddenly the place started filling with water until the two men lost their carbide lamps and found themselves treading water to keep from drowning in the dark. At last, after some hours, the water receded and they escaped. You can imagine why such an experience might cause a person to forbid his son that path in life.

Stu attended Kansas University but not to study mining or engineering or even geology. He graduated with a degree in Sociology, a field that I think never again held any interest for him.

Becky Fahrig, marching down the aisle in January 1940, may have felt she was marrying an American version of Denis Passadoro, whose business card, carefully pasted into her scrapbook reads (in Italian) "Director General of 'His Master's Voice – Columbia – Marconiphone.'" Well, at least Stuart looked like him – when he took off his glasses.

It was a large, elaborate wedding, and less than a year after her return from kissing Denis goodbye in Italy. The Fahrigs were a popular family in Joplin as well as in the DuPont universe, plus there had been a lot of local newsprint about Becky's trip to Italy, and soon wedding gifts and congratulations streamed in.

In all the excitement, Becky found herself under a lot of tension and her weight fell to 101 pounds. She experienced a moment of panic in the week before her wedding. She thought, "I don't remember what he looks like!" It revealed an existential truth – she and Stu were almost complete strangers. In fact, their wedding day would be only the second time they'd see each other in the daylight.

One wonders what the conversation was as this photo was taken of the bride with her parents. "Why such haste?" Seems an obvious question. And "Are you sure, Dear?" Although, judging by the expression on her face, Becky's mind was made up.

On the afternoon of January 28, 1940, the First Presbyterian Church of Joplin, seating 600 and beautifully decorated with flowers and candles, was packed. It was "The Wedding of The Year" according to the Joplin Globe. Becky was a local celebrity by dint of her famous trip to

Italy with her sister. They had returned only eleven months earlier. The organ swung into Mendelssohn's *Wedding March* and Harry Fahrig offered his arm to his favorite child and escorted her down the aisle. She wore her grandmother Short's beautifully refurbished wedding gown. Stu, waiting at the altar with Rod as his best man, was sorry he had obeyed her wish and put his eyeglasses in his pocket.

"Damn it, Rod," he muttered, "I can't see her!"

"Well, Stu," Rod replied, "Do you want me to point?"

After the exchange of holy vows, Becky was only too happy to take Stu's arm and lead him down the aisle and into the uncertain future. They left the church to the strains of *Somewhere Over the Rainbow*.

Becky and Stu were still children in some respects. Years later, she told her daughter Mimi that on their wedding night they had a "wet washcloth fight!" It's easy to imagine two youngsters on their wedding trip, after a long drive, in a strange motel, would feel the need to break the tension like a pair of siblings by letting their abundant energies out in a mock battle. The giggles soon settled into a loving embrace. Becky once said, "Yes, we were strangers at first, but the more we learned about each other, the more we liked."

At first the Conoco job meant days apart from each other. There were many trips from their small apartment in El Paso to distant towns on the train. Until, one fateful journey traveling with company superiors, Stu made a business suggestion that did not please them. He found himself fired and standing on a station platform in New Mexico, paying the fare back to Becky in El Paso. Then came a series of dead-end jobs for less and less money. At one point Becky's father got him a job as a salesman for du Pont, but Stu was unhappy in a corporate setting and quit. By this time, they were living in Georgia and Alabama while Stu was seeking factory work for poor wages.

It's important to remember that marriage in 1940 was a far more serious commitment than it would become even thirty years later. Divorce was quite rare in their generation and frowned on by the conservative social rules of their time.

There was also a story she told from that early time of an argument she and her new husband had that ended with them angrily walking down opposite sides of the street. Perhaps she had offered to find work herself or talked once too often about a wonderful event in Italy. Either of those topics could hit a sensitive nerve in Stu, Becky learned. She would put the scrapbook away and, while often a volunteer, she would never hold a paying job in her life. Stu was a proud man and would have been hurt and angered by the suggestion that he couldn't fulfill his role.

It's possible this argument was a turning point of their marriage when they worked out the rules of their relationship. We can only guess about the private and personal bargain of their long and successful relationship. Italy had been a winning streak for her. Denis had been her trophy. Now, she was faced with a difficult challenge. Stu did not know how to win yet, but she did.

That frightened young man striding angrily on the other side of the street was her husband, and she saw that only she could give him the encouragement he needed. She decided to be his partner. She thought of her own parents and the way they loved and respected each other. How each of them had their own accomplishments and skills. She saw the way to support Stu was to believe in his dream. To share that dream. What was his dream? She didn't know, but she was determined to find out and help him achieve it. I think that's when Becky crossed the street and took his hand.

The biggest problem of the early years of their marriage was the fact that Stu had no reliable profession even though he had a BA from the University of Kansas. In 1940, the country remained in the grip of the Depression when the only jobs to be had were factory jobs at poor wages. They moved around the southern states starting in Texas, then to Georgia and Alabama. When World War Two began after Pearl Harbor in 1941, Stu tried to enlist in the Army but was rejected because of his poor eyesight. A year later, in December of 1942, while he was working in a factory in Birmingham, Alabama, Becky gave birth to me, their first child. She named me Michael Fahrig Landrum after hearing a radio show that mentioned the archangel Michael, and she thought it was a fine name.

Research tells us that in February 1943, RAF Flight Lieutenant Denis J Passadoro was killed in an air crash at El Adam Airport in Libya; he was one of twelve passengers who died on the Lockheed Hudson plane. Cause of crash was listed as engine failure, not foul play, nor enemy fire. Denis had gotten married on 22 June 1942 at St Joseph's (RC), Cairo, to Miss Suzanne née Easton of Durban. He was an intelligence officer in the Royal Air Force.

In April of 1943 the army relented and allowed Stu to enlist. He was stationed at La Jolla, California and was assigned

Becky with Mike

as company clerk for an infantry training unit. When the unit shipped out to join the battles in the Pacific, he managed to persuade his Capitan that he was more valuable staying stateside as a training company clerk. It was one of the first signs of his true talent – he could be a persuasive salesman. In October 1944, while he was stationed at Fort Bliss, Texas near El Paso, Becky gave birth to their second son. They named him Stuart Milton Landrum, Jr. nicknamed Mitty.

After the War and his discharge from the army, they decided to follow Stu's dream of finding riches as his father had, in the mining industry. So, they chose Colorado and moved to Steamboat Springs, deep in the Rocky Mountains where Stu could prospect for minerals in his spare time. He found work to pay the bills by becoming a bulk gasoline truck driver for Mobil Oil. They built a small house on the edge of town, and Becky filled her hours tending her little ones and learning the art of oil painting from a correspondence course.

After three years and no luck prospecting and bad luck driving the gasoline truck, they moved back to Baxter Springs, Kansas. Wes Landrum helped his son buy a franchise from Meadow Gold Milk and Stu became a deliveryman for milk and eggs. Becky and the boys were happy in Baxter where there were many friends and family. With Stu working for himself in a business that was steady and secure, only eighteen miles from Joplin and the Fahrigs, Becky happily defined this period as the "white bread" of her life.

But the dream of mining was still alive in Stu, and in January 1951, the family moved to Fredericktown, Missouri where he became personnel director for the National Lead mine there. They bought a house on West Main Street and Becky gave it a complete redesign. In 1952 she felt confident and happy enough to have a third child, thus, her daughter Rebecca Ann Landrum was born in November 1952. Becky nicknamed her 'Mimi,' like the heroine of La Boehme. But since that powerful experience of first seeing the opera with Denis in Milan was one of her many private memories, Becky never told Stu or her family about it.

Perhaps it was bringing Mimi into her life that stimulated Becky to reawaken the spirit of her year of glory as the toast of Milano. But how could she be the Americanata in America? How could she find that happy, creative confidence she had felt in a great city of Europe, while living in Fredericktown, Missouri? Was the great "education of travel" that her parents had so generously provided now simply to shrivel and die in an obscure backwoods' town in Southeast Missouri?

Becky had indeed become a "Woman of the World." While Fredericktown, population 2500, may not be the equal of a great city of

Europe, still, it was part of the same world. It could be that all the fascinating men and women she had met between Joplin and Italy, added up to fewer than 2500. Fredericktown may only be a tiny patch in the Ozarks, but they were the same sort of human beings as the rich and famous she had met. As Harry Fahrig might put it, "They all put their pants on one leg at a time." Fredericktown had society, too.

Becky joined that society with the gracious attitude that she had learned from Mrs. Johnston in New York City. She made new friends with the same selfless focus that her dear sister Harriet had shown when leading her and Blossom around the room of strangers to shake every hand.

Becky & Mimi

As the extroverted half of the couple, she inspired her husband to join her and become leaders of their social circle in the creation a "Golf and Country Club." That was where she and Stu put on hilarious skits, raising money for worthy causes, and just for fun. 'Americanata' had become

Becky's enthusiastic and positive point of view helping her new community ride happily over any dreariness she came across. Becky took to golf, and new friends appeared in foursomes. Golf quickly became one of her dearest passions. It was a place to strive, to always work for self-improvement. She racked up three Hole-in-Ones. She loved learning and growing. She also continued to paint and study the arts and produced dozens of canvases.

Meanwhile, Stu was having trouble at work. The market for lead was declining, leaded paint soon gave way to latex, and the wages of miners suffered. Stu found himself in battles with the miners' union threatening strikes, and the company in New York refused to raise wages. By 1957 he'd had enough as the man in the middle of an intractable dispute and, with Becky's strong encouragement, he quit the mining business for something new.

Stu discovered insurance, something he could believe in and sell. He bought a small State Farm agency in nearby Farmington, Missouri. At last, at the age of 42, Stu Landrum had found his calling in a business working for himself. Farmington, eighteen miles closer to St Louis, was on the cusp of becoming a small city of 3500 people and growing. With Becky's full support and encouragement, they both became leaders in the social life of their new community. Becky joined the Garden Club and launched projects for the beautification of the town. There were book clubs, bridge clubs and of course, another golf club where they socialized to beat the band.

In Farmington they continued to function as a Power Couple. She had found her milieu, a social atmosphere like the one she had experienced in the homes and clubs of Milan, though on a modest, American middle-class level. The social skills she had developed in Italy continued to carry them forward in their new community.

Stu, freed now from the headaches of trying to control a bunch of angry miners, made friends with the businessmen of his new town. He joined the Rotary Club and mingled with community leaders. He soon sold the State Farm agency and bought out an older, well-established insurance office. He became independent, more interested in the larger game of insurance and community development. Farmington was <u>his</u>

community. He became chairman of the Chamber of Commerce and launched a campaign to build a badly needed regional hospital; then he led the effort to create a new campus for the local junior college, renaming it Mineral Area College. The Landrum Insurance business grew and eventually he expanded it to include his son, Mit. The grateful city fathers and the chamber honored him as "Man of the Year." A few years later they would give Becky a Matching award, "Woman of the Year."

While I was a child for most of this period, and had no awareness of their negotiations, here is what I could observe from my parents' behavior. They each had their own areas of power and control. Stu was the sole breadwinner; Becky ran the household and eventually became the dominant parent. They never argued in front of us kids. Fidelity was mutual and solid; each of them swore full allegiance, respect, and support for one another. I remember during the early years of struggle, Mother telling me and my brother, "Your father is the finest man!"

There was one further proviso, perhaps never stated but understood by Becky: she refrained from telling Stu about her wonderful year in Italy. She put away her souvenirs and the trip diary; they became her private joy. She did not bring them out until 1997 when, after 57 years of happily married life together, Stu Landrum died. Then, at the age of 80, she brought them out and enlisted me, her eldest child, to help her with the writing as she shared with the world that magic year in Italy. After more than sixty years, her many memories of Italy remained vivid.

Becky Fahrig Landrum lived the rest of her life in Farmington, Missouri, a much-loved cultural figure of the area. She became a leader of every club she ever belonged to and was the matriarch of her large and growing family with six grandchildren and nine great grandchildren so far. In her 80's she was asked to manage a local farmer's market, and around that time the local AM Radio station offered her a weekly morning slot to host a talk show. With her dear friend Anne Ledbetter, they put on a half hour program they called "Our Two Cents," discussing local events and interviewing people of the area. When her memoir *Americanata* was self-published in 2001, she hosted a series of "Signing Parties" and spoke the remembered glory and the looming threat of 1938 Italy.

Becky on Center St, Farmington, MO

Becky Fahrig Landrum was a strong parent and graceful social leader. She applied the skills she first learned from her mother and Mrs. Johnston in New York, then, as a member of Harriet's busy household, she was able to practice and grow as a socialite in Milan with her sisters. Her mother had been right about travel – she had left Joplin a girl and returned a more mature and confident woman of the world.

When she finally passed away at age 95 on December 4, 2012, the largest church in Farmington was as packed with friends as the church in Joplin that had witnessed her wedding. She was loved and respected by every level of her society from the six State Troopers who carried her casket, to the members of the motorcycle gang who befriended her at the Farmer's Market. She was a strong Christian believer and church member. When she died, my brother, Mit delivered her eulogy. I'll always remember her as she once described herself, "Happy on purpose!"

The story of her family, which is her proudest accomplishment will have to wait for another book.

The Landrum Family - Christmas 1994

Eulogy

Becky Landrum was born Rebecca Ann Fahrig on April 11, 1917, in the little mining town of Ramsey, Montana. She was the fourth and last child of Harry and Florence Short Fahrig and the sister of Harriet, Richard and Blossom. Her father Harry worked as an engineer for the du Pont Chemical Co. Ramsey was a little town near the open pit mines of Butte, and a lot of dynamite was used in the mine, so Granddaddy Fahrig was du Pont's man in the field. Shortly after momma's birth, the family moved to Washburn, Wisconsin on the shores of Lake Superior. Her father was transferred to Joplin in 1925 where momma grew up and graduated from High School.

A highlight of her early experience was in 1938 when she and her sister Blossom spent a year in Italy, visiting their elder sister Harriet who had married an Italian and was raising a family in Milan. Momma recorded her experiences in her memoir *Americanata* which she wrote with the help of my brother Mike.

Back from Italy, she met Stuart M. Landrum on a blind date. It was love at first sight – Pop proposed after only a month or so, and he went back to his job for an oil company in New Mexico. Momma made wedding arrangements. Time passed, and as the day approached it occurred to momma that she could not remember exactly what pop looked like – they had dated mostly at night. But all was well when he got back to Joplin for the wedding, and they married on Jan 28, 1940. They were together for 57 years, raising three kids – Rebecca, Mike and me.

Momma wanted to be a good wife, so early on she learned that Pop loved pie. As soon as they settled into their first place in Bremen, GA, momma created her first pie. Looking back, the pie was a total disaster, the rubbery crust had floated about half way up to the surface, and the rest of the pie was pretty bad as well. Momma described the crust as being about a half inch think and so rubbery that you could flex it back and forth ten or twelve times without cracking it, but Pop didn't want to discourage her and manned-up. Every day when he came home from work, he would take the pie down from the top of the ice-box and pronounce, "Well, guess I'll have another whack at the pie." And he would have a piece and put it right back up. It was only some time later that it occurred to momma that she should have simply thrown the pie out. Instead, he just kept coming back for another "whack" until the he had eaten the whole thing.

Like almost every other American man, our father went into the army in World War II, and served until VJ day in 1945. And like everybody else, he was looking for work after the war. We lived in For Morgan, CO, Steamboat Springs, CO, Baxter Springs, KS, and finally in 1952, we moved to Fredericktown, MO.

Momma's father had died in 1951, she was about to have Rebecca, and she was looking for answers. She was always a reader, and she found a book called *The Sermon on the Mount*, by Emmet Fox that just resonated with her. It came to her in a moment of pure inspiration that she could actually control the happiness of her own life by the thoughts that she had. She could choose how she thought about anything, and that she was not a helpless victim of circumstance – times might be difficult; trouble might come, but she could choose to find something good in it regardless. I was eight at the time, but I can remember when she decided that she would face life in a new way.

It made perfect sense... Why not choose to live the best life you could? She used to say, "When you lay down on your death bed, you'll have a lifetime good memories to look back on."

What she didn't realize then was that when she chose a lifetime of good memories for herself, she also chose a lifetime of providing good memories to us.

It was a gift she gave each person she met.

I know you are thinking back to memories you have of momma – here are a few of ours…

- Most of you know that momma was an avid golfer, but did you know that she kept a five iron in the kitchen, a five wood in the sunroom, and seven iron in the bedroom? She had the seven-iron upstairs because the ceilings were lower and she needed a shorter club. She would be struck by some new "swing thought", and she didn't want to be too far from a golf club that she could grab and groove her swing. Pop woke up in the middle of the night one time to see momma at the foot of  the bed swinging the seven-iron. She took a chunk of linoleum out of the kitchen floor once – that was a bad swing-thought, apparently.

- Speaking of golf, she had a pair of bifocals with the lenses reversed so the distance vision was at the bottom so she could see the ball at address. This worked pretty well except when she marked her score card – she had to hold the card up over her head because near vision was now at the top.

- Back in the 1960's she taught Sunday school at the Presbyterian Church, and her class was mostly kids from the Home for Children. One Sunday she taught her class, and then went to church. After church we went outside to discover that our car had been stolen by her Sunday School class! The police finally located the car and the kids down in the Boot heel, and the car was totaled after a high-speed chase, but it was a long time before we let her forget about how effective she was as a Sunday School teacher.

- In the early 1950's we our house in Fredericktown had a large front yard, and this soon become the play ground for my brother and my self along with a lot of other boys in the neighborhood. And, of course, we pretty well tore the yard up. One of momma's friends pointed out to her how badly the yard looked and that it was too bad that the kids were tearing it up. Momma simply replied that it didn't bother her one bit. She said, "I'm not growing grass this year; I'm growing boys."

- In 1967 my brother Mike was drafted and received orders to go to Viet Nam. When he called and told her that he had to go, her response was "Well, isn't it nice that you'll be able to see that part of the world!" At first that seems so unreal, but it was just her way of dealing with this terrible unsettling news; she was trying to recast this into something positive.

- She was always telling us stuff, and if we didn't like what she was saying, she would say, "Well, yes, but you'll change". After a while this became a family joke. She actually meant that as an encouragement. Momma never fought change; to her change meant opportunity. Change meant new things to learn. As she grew older, she believed every decade was better than the previous one. When she hit 50, it was good because she had left a lot of youthful anxiety behind; when she hit 60 she and Pop had more freedom to travel. And so forth. I know what you're thinking... What about when she turned 90? She said, "you know, I can say whatever I want, and what are they going to do? I'm an old lady."

The center of her life was her love for people.

Her formula was uncomplicated and childlike... It may surprise you to know that momma didn't set out to have any of you as a friend at all. She set out to be your friend. A friend would never allow another friend to suffer the anxiety of trying join in socially, so, if you were a stranger, she would seek you out. A friend always sees the best in another friend, so as she came forward to introduce herself, she would have already decided to like you. A friend is interested in the life of another friend, so as she spoke with you, she would listen and ask about you. A friend cares about another friend, and she would pour out encouragement and love at every opportunity.

And so she has gone home to her loving maker, but still, she lives with us.

- She lives in every kind word and generous act.
- She lives in every moment of welcome and acceptance that she brought to a stranger.
- She lives in every comfort and encouragement she lavished on every one of us.
- She lives in every good memory she decided so long ago to keep, but wound up giving away to all of us and countless people no longer here.

She was living proof that it is not the material wealth, or fame, or earthly glory in life that counts, but what you are inside.

Thank God, thank God almighty, it is not good bye forever, it is only good bye for now.

Momma, unforgettable, loving momma -

I love you forever Momma. Forever.

Mit

Stuart M. Landrum, Jr

Made in the USA
Middletown, DE
01 August 2024

58365771R00133